HELP! MY CHURCH IS LEAVING ME

Adapting to a Changing UMC

EDITED BY BILL KEMP

WITH CHAPTERS BY: DARRELL COATS   JOE FORT

ROGER GRACE   BILL KEMP   KATHY MOORE

NOT PERFECT YET Publishing

Why this book?

You may feel like a penguin on an ice flow drifting away from the fellowship you love. The question is not whether you are on solid ground and the church adrift, or vice versa.

The question is:

> *How do you discern the will of God and learn to live compassionately in this moment?*

This book takes the reader behind the scenes of the LGBTQ debate in the United Methodist Church. It teaches spiritual discernment, listening skills, and small group process while encouraging the differing sides of the issue to rediscover their unity in Christ.

> *We each must learn how to pray without prejudice and to make church decisions without bias.*

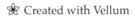 Created with Vellum

Contents

Introduction

Jesus says, "Give unto Caesar what is Caesar's..." We all nod our heads. Wouldn't it be nice if we could leave both current culture and divisive politics to the weekday and have our worship time uncluttered by social concerns? Yet every week, it seems, some ethical challenge or political cause gets mentioned in church. Has your church bulletin ever invited people to attend a "Right to Life" rally? Is there interest in serving as a sanctuary for undocumented immigrants? Have you ever lost a member because he disagreed with the pastor's politics? Like it or not, social issues already impact your congregational life.

Over the last three decades, the world outside the church has undergone a rapid shift in its acceptance of both homosexuality and gender identity issues. Every four years, a General Conference representing all United Methodists gathers and spends hours debating which parts of our church law (*The Book of Discipline*) need to be changed to keep pace with new understandings about human sexuality and other social issues. Some congregations and individuals wish that the United Methodist Church was out in front leading change rather than reacting to it. Others fear that we've already lost our Wesleyan soul by failing to preach holiness in opposition to the sexual deviance of our era. The two sides are no longer merely drifting apart. They have raised sail and have charted separate destinations for the congregations they lead.

Consider a penguin on an ice floe. The fellowship to which she belongs can be seen drifting away from her. She may feel that her own position remains unchanged and that the church is at fault for moving. But could it be that the church is on solid ground and it is the penguin who is being drawn by unseen forces into uncharted territory? Who is leaving whom? Is it just a matter of perspective? Help! Our relationship with each other is changing and we don't know why.

Help! My Church is Leaving Me is written by United Methodist Church leaders who are trained in the art of congregational transition. Transition differs from mere change in that it is usually initiated by a trauma or change in status that radically alters our sense of identity. Getting married is a transition; buying a new car is not. To use a biblical analogy, when the flood came and Noah took his family into an ark, they were involved in a transition. Before the flood, their identity was that of one family living in the midst of a wider civilization. During the flood, they found themselves struggling to understand their new role as zookeepers. They emerged from the flood, not just as survivors, but as a people "set apart" to build something new.

The rains have been falling on the United Methodist denomination for a long time. The flood waters have risen. Conventional means to drain the controversy have failed. In February of 2019, delegates to the specially called General Conference of the United Methodist Church stood before a number of competing arks. By a narrow vote, the Traditional Plan emerged as the only approved way forward. But what about the people who are unwilling to step on that boat, or not allowed to continue in church leadership because they are LGBTQ (Lesbian, Gay, Bisexual, Transgendered, or otherwise Questioning/Queer)? Are other means for being Methodist available for them? On or off this Traditional Plan boat, church leadership will have a "zookeeper" feel to it for the foreseeable future. How do we keep people from devouring each other with hurtful language? What ministries, mission work, and resources will we lose? Is it time to put out a life raft and look for survivors? What will the church look like in ten years?

Trauma & Transition

Do you find your own relationship with the United Methodist Church undergoing a transition? What about your congregation? Consider the following trauma indicators:

1. The pastor and/or other significant leaders may desire to take the church in a particular direction but fail to get the needed support.

2. You or your current pastor may have strong feelings about who can be married in your sanctuary. You may be wondering how the decision to define marriage only as between a man and a woman will change your congregation's relationship with those who are able to be married elsewhere.

3. Most people in your congregation may misunderstand or

be baffled by the decisions being made by the denomination. Many are asking if the Traditional Plan is the final word on the subject. Are we still in motion or have we found a resting place?

4. Those who do understand the denomination and have read extensively about the issues may be wishing that the General Church had added more teeth to its decision. They ask, "Why are we allowing liberals to run our seminaries and mission agencies?"

5. Others, just as knowledgeable, may be in mourning for the people we are now excluding from leadership, and for the couples whose relationship we will no longer honor.

6. Loss of members and income on account of these issues is already affecting your church.

7. The acceptance of the Traditional Plan is causing many clergy persons and church staff to reconsider their loyalty to the United Methodist denomination. Your congregation may be forced into an undesired leadership change.

8. A critical mass may be forming in your congregation for exiting the denomination.

We live in a society divided by fake news, immoderate speech, and the tendency for each of us to listen only to the people we already agree with. This is often referred to as the "filter bubble" (see Chapter Three). What is happening in your local church mirrors what is happening outside. Political polarization in the secular world is spilling over, driving missional apathy, membership loss, and the possibility of church schism. People feel strongly. For some, it's about justice that's been too long denied. For others, it's about a moral stance too quickly being abandoned. If only we could have a sanctuary on Sunday in which to hide and recover. No matter what our church leaders have decided, homosexuality and gender identity issues will continue to be hot topics at our family gatherings, at our workplaces, and on the fields where our children and sports heroes compete. It would be odd for the church to simply ignore these issues.

Note the following:

• Despite advocating a separation of sacred and secular, Jesus managed to get himself sentenced to death by both the priesthood and the political powers.

• The early church was persecuted by both religious and civic authorities.

• Things became even more muddled when the Emperor Constantine decided to join the church and give Christianity state approval.

• Both Luther's reformation and Wesley's revival changed the world by changing the church.

• Religious thought and church involvement in social causes have significantly changed everyday life, as well as our political process.

• It is a myth to think that we can go back to some simpler past when social issues were less divisive.

So, you may feel like a penguin on an ice floe drifting away from the fellowship you love. The question is not whether you are on solid ground and the church adrift, or vice versa. The question is:

How do you discern the will of God
and learn to live compassionately in this moment?

Process & Discernment

It used to be that when people said, "The church is getting too political," they meant that the process for making decisions and allocating money was too often influenced by a few powerful people. Today, when people worry about the church being political they mean that the church is being split by the same divisions — left versus right — that we see in our nation. Both viewpoints relate to the church not being Christ-like. That said, the way back to aligning the church with Christ's teachings and becoming fully engaged with the mission he has for it, lies in both improving our congregation's political process and our individual capacity for spiritual discernment. Simply put, we each must learn how to pray without prejudice and to make church decisions without bias.

This book offers a twofold solution:

- Some of the chapters are process oriented and focused on how to make unbiased personal and congregational decisions.
- Other chapters are reflective and meant to teach how to pray without prejudice.

The chapters in this book are self-contained units and you are invited to read them in any order. In most chapters, group study questions are marked with an asterisk,* inviting you to study and reflect with an open mind. These are often difficult questions, but talking about them with other people might just open up your relationship with others and strengthen the group process of your congregation. The actual order of the chapters has been chosen with small group development in mind. It begins with hearing and thinking, then moves toward speech and action. The early chapters build the relational infrastructure for the more difficult chapters that follow.

2019

This book was compiled in the weeks following the Special General Conference in St. Louis. It contains some early predictions as to what the effect of the Traditional Plan will be on local church life. The plan is to periodically update the book's quarterly editions over the next two years. These changes will be annotated in a resource article at www.notperfectyet.com.

None of the authors represent an "official" view. Bill Kemp, as editor, has avoided interviewing the leading voices on both sides of the issue. Instead, he has invited lesser known writers who each can present one segment with clarity, balance, and integrity. The authors are a diverse group, but united in the hope that you and your congregation will be sustained by the Holy Spirit and encouraged by our words as you transition through the wilderness that lies before the United Methodist Church. And yes, it is a wilderness (see Chapter Five). Taking a vote in St. Louis has not brought us instantly into the Promised Land. Nor did it reverse the course of the whole denomination and set our GPS to a bygone era. No, it is to use a neutral term, a wilderness period. God's church can learn a lot from this segment of the journey.

The purpose of this book, again, is not to argue the issues. It is instead to encourage you as a participant in your congregation and in whatever leadership capacity you have, to be less anxious. As the Bible often says, "be unafraid." The church is still "of God, and will be preserved to the end of time, for the conduct of worship..."[1]

ONE

What Just Happened?

BY ROGER GRACE

A special session of the General Conference of the United Methodist Church was held February 23-26, 2019, in St. Louis, Missouri. Its single focus was to find a way forward amid our church's divided policies regarding human sexuality, relating to homosexual practice and marriage covenants, as well as gender identity. In terms of general church law, the guiding rule has long been "The practice of homosexuality is incompatible with Christian teaching" (Paragraph 304.3, The 2016 United Methodist Book of Discipline). This line is the foundation for a series of ordinances preventing self-declared, practicing homosexuals from receiving ordination and any clergy person from participating in a marriage or civil ceremony that recognizes a same-sex union.

A large percentage of United Methodist church members no longer believe that homosexuality is incompatible with Christianity. Meanwhile in American society, discrimination against LGBTQ people is considered immoral by many and illegal in certain contexts. Age is sometimes a divider with these issues, with many younger adults rejecting current church doctrine and a lot of older persons upholding what are considered to be traditional values. Ethnicity, life experience, and location are also polarizing factors. Many rural people are more inclined to dismiss gender identity issues, unless they personally have a family member or an acquaintance who is transgendered or questioning.

Meanwhile, over 800 United Methodist congregations have declared themselves to be "Reconciling Churches." They refuse to teach, or by their non-participation indicate, that homosexuality is in any way incompatible with Christianity. Several United Methodist conferences have also placed themselves in opposition to church law by ordaining practicing homosexuals and refusing to prosecute clergy who participate in same-sex weddings. Then in 2016, a bishop who has a same-sex spouse was elected to serve in the Pacific Northwest Jurisdiction. On the other hand, a significant number of United Methodist church leaders have joined the Wesleyan Covenant Association, which has threatened to form a breakaway denomination if the general church doesn't act to uphold the relevant paragraphs of the *Book of Discipline.*

At the 2016 General Conference, the Council of Bishops was tasked with prayerfully seeking a way out of this impasse. They formed the "Commission on a Way Forward," which brought to the Special General Conference a number of plans to resolve these issues.

The plans presented by the Commission on the Way Forward were:

1) **The One Church Plan** - which would have allowed

Annual Conferences and Jurisdictions to decide for themselves whether to ordain practicing LGBTQ candidates for ministry and whether clergy could participate in weddings or unions of LGBTQ couples. The One Church Plan was supported by a majority of the Council of Bishops.

2) **The Connectional Conference Plan** - would have created several connectional sub-units within the whole of the United Methodist church, allowing the rules to be different in different places. The Connectional Conference Plan would have required a series of Constitutional Amendments to be implemented and thus was considered by many to be untenable.

These first two plans failed to gain a majority vote at the Special General Conference.

3) **The Traditional Plan** - was adopted, strengthening the existing language of the Discipline and adding further account-ability on the part of Bishops, Clergy, and Boards of Ordained Ministry.

Another idea, **The Simple Plan**, came from an outside orga-nization. It proposed simply removing any language from the *Book of Discipline* that related to LGBTQ or same-sex issues in the church. That would have allowed each church, Annual Confer-ence, Jurisdiction, or Episcopal Area, to choose how to deal with those topics.

Components of the Traditional plan, especially enforcement language regarding the current relationship of clergy persons who are LGBTQ, are under review as of the publication of this book. Future editions and the www.notperfectyet.com website will provide updates. A separate piece of legislation which was passed suggests that local churches will be given the right to take their property with them if they choose to join another denomination or withdraw from the United Methodist Church following the 2020 General Conference. That so-called "Gracious Exit" plan is also being reviewed by the Judicial Council to determine if it is constitutional.

Q & A

Bill Kemp, this book's editor, submitted to Roger Grace the following ten questions as a way to help unpack what all of the above might mean for your congregation.

Question 1: *You were a delegate to the 2019 Special General Conference. Can you say something about the processes you and the other delegates went through as you prepared to make the difficult deci-sions that were entrusted to you at that gathering?*

While I cannot speak for all delegates, I can give you an over-view of what I did to try to prepare. Obviously, I read all the official pre-conference mailings that were sent to us. The "Advance Daily Christian Advocate" had the full plans that were presented.[1] ADCA also listed all the petitions that were sent by individual United Methodists and UM related organizations. There were 49 petitions related to the three plans presented by the Commission on the Way Forward and an additional 50 from other entities. The planning process was complicated, since the Judicial Council ruled that 21 of the additional 50 petitions that were included in the ADCA were unconstitutional or "not in harmony" with the stated purpose of the called general confer-ence. Those petitions that were not in harmony were not addressed by the conference. Those that were unconstitutional had to be amended in order to become constitutional. Some were dealt with and some were not.

In addition to all the official materials that were distributed, I read the postings by *Good News* and other more traditional publications as well as those by the Reconciling Ministries Network and the Uniting Methodists or Centrist movement. I wanted to hear as many differing opinions as possible as I tried to discern what my response to the issues would be in St. Louis.

Our West Ohio Conference Delegation also had several different meetings as we discussed the plans before us in prepa-ration for the gathering. Our Bishop led a series of Question and Answer sessions around the Annual Conference, in which the various plans were presented. Laity and clergy were given the opportunity to let the Bishop and the delegates know what their thinking was on the three major plans. Many hours were spent in preparation for this General Conference.

QUESTION 2: *WHEN THERE ARE DISCUSSIONS IN THE LOCAL CHURCH about LGBTQ issues, what do people at the grass roots level need to know about United Methodist beliefs and practices?*

Now that is a loaded question. The 2016 *Book of Discipline* states in part: "We affirm that all persons are individuals of sacred worth, created in the image of God..."[2] Then it goes on to say, "The United Methodist Church does not condone the practice of homosexuality and considers this practice incompatible with Christian teaching." This "incompatibility" statement was added to the 1972 *Book of Discipline* in the Social Principles section, which is not considered to be UMC law. Rather, "[The Social Principles] are a call to faithfulness and are intended to be instructive and persuasive in the best of the prophetic spirit."[3] Later General Conferences started adding the words to other portions of the *Book of Discipline* dealing with the ordination of "self-avowed, practicing homosexuals" as well as prohibitions against United Methodist clergy performing or participating in same-sex unions or marriages. There is nothing in the *Book of Discipline* that says LGBTQ persons cannot be members of the UMC or serve in local church leadership.

That said, there is wide variance across the denomination in how churches and individuals live out and practice their beliefs. Just as some areas of the United States are more open and accepting of differences between people, so too there are United Methodist Churches that are more open and accepting of sexual differences. To complicate matters, since the UMC is a world-wide church, we also need to be aware of and factor in the differing understandings about sexuality across the globe. For instance, in some countries, homosexuality is a crime and the penalty could be a death sentence. That is far different from the U.S. where gay marriage is now legal.

QUESTION 3: *ARE YOU AFRAID THAT THE DECISION TO BACK THE Traditional Plan will cause an exodus of young, educated, and/or urban people from the United Methodist Church?*

I know that there is a perception that progressives are for the most part young, educated, and/or urban, but I believe that is a misconception. There are many who are progressive who are maybe a bit older, possibly less-educated, and/or rural. This issue is less about young vs. old, educated vs. uneducated, or urban vs. rural than it is about biblical interpretation. How do we read, understand, and interpret the Bible?

I do not believe, at this time, that there will be a major exodus of the more "progressive" branch of the UMC due to the adoption of the Traditional Plan. Its adoption may well generate more protest, more disobedience to the prohibitions against performing same-sex weddings, and more District Committees and Conference Boards of Ordained Ministry approving the candidacy of LGBTQ persons who come before them. The Traditional Plan was approved by only 54 out of about 820 votes cast (53%-47%). This could embolden those in the church who are working towards more inclusivity. I expect them to ramp up their resistance to the tightening restrictions on LGBTQ participation in the life of the church. Yet while I don't see a mass migration out of the church at this time, I do believe that in the

US, many of those not yet in the church may choose to take a second look before committing to a church that is considered by many to be unwelcoming and judgmental of LGBTQ persons.

QUESTION 4: *BEFORE THE SPECIAL GENERAL CONFERENCE MET, WERE you concerned that the One Church plan might cause an exodus of older, less-educated, and/or rural people from the United Methodist Church?*

Again, as in the previous question, I believe that this has less to do with age, education, or place than it does about biblical understanding and interpretation. I do believe that those who have a more traditional understanding and interpretation of the scripture are potentially more likely to withdraw from the UMC if a different understanding or interpretation gains broader acceptance. Part of the reason I think that is because the Wesleyan Covenant Association has the structure in place to create a new Methodist/Wesleyan denomination that is based upon their understanding and interpretation of the biblical witness. If the Judicial Council rules that the "Gracious Exit" plan approved at St. Louis is constitutional, then the means would be in place for local churches, Annual Conferences, and even Jurisdictions to withdraw from the United Methodist Church with their properties, under certain circumstances. That could lead to a large exodus from the UMC.

[NOTE: *KEY ELEMENTS OF THE TRADITIONAL PLAN AND THE "Gracious Exit" provision were ruled constitutional at the April 2019 meeting of the Judicial Council.*]

Question 5: *Do you have any thoughts about how Christians should behave in today's polarized political environment?*

I believe that the Golden Rule is a good place to start: treat others as we would like to be treated. It seems to me that there is less willingness than there has been in the past to listen to those whose beliefs differ from our own, so really listening to others to learn not just what they believe but also why they believe it, is a step in the right direction. I do some conflict resolution work and one of the tools that I use is to encourage people to speak about how actions affect them personally: that is, how they feel, not speaking in second or third person, but identifying how a conflict situation impacts them. When we do that, we may actually feel their pain and gain some understanding of why they believe as they do, even if we disagree with their beliefs. Truly listening to someone is a sign of respect, and many problems might be resolved if mutual respect is shown to one another.

QUESTION 6: *WHAT ADVICE WOULD YOU GIVE TO PASTORS AND PPRC committees when they meet in private with exploring candidates for ministry who may have misgivings about the United Methodist Church's position on LGBTQ issues?*

When persons sense a call from God to become a minister and come before the Pastor Parish Relations Committee (PPRC) for examination and a recommendation to enter the candidacy process, they should have at least a rudimentary understanding of Chapter 2 of the *Book of Discipline*. This chapter deals with the ministry of all Christians as well as with those who are set apart for specialized ministry. Those entering ministry, as well as the PPRC, should know the Qualifications for Ordination found in paragraph 304. This paragraph is the one that lays out all the requirements for credentials in the UMC and includes the restrictive language regarding the ordination of practicing homosexuals. Candidates who are "straight" should know that those who are actively "gay" are currently not to be considered by Boards of Ordained Ministry for ordination. Are the straight candidates willing to uphold the disciplinary prohibitions against credentialing active LGBTQ persons? If any candidates are actively living in an LGBTQ relationship, they need to be aware of the hurdles ahead of them in their quest for ministry in the UMC.

In reality, different annual conferences apply the *Book of Discipline* in a variety of ways. Some have stated that they are going to defy the prohibitions. They plan to welcome all who are otherwise qualified for ministry without regard to their sexual orientation. Currently there is one Jurisdiction in the US that is openly defiant as well as one Conference in a Central Conference that has announced that it will not abide by the exclusions mandated by the *Book of Discipline*. In those settings, the PPRC will probably have different advice for a candidate than in the areas that continue to enforce the *Book of Discipline*. PPRC members and their pastors need to be aware of the circumstances in which they live and serve in order to provide appropriate guidance for new candidates for ministry.

QUESTION 7: *SOME CLERGY PERSONS AND CHURCH STAFF FIND themselves in opposition to where the denomination is headed. What advice would you give to them? Are there things they should do before making any decision that affects their career?*

This question is a double-edged sword, I think. People on both sides of the debate over LGBTQ come at it from a passionate belief that their understanding is correct and is within God's plan for how the church should be the church. There are many on the more traditional side who feel that if the UMC changes and accepts LGBTQ persons into ordination and approves of same-sex weddings, they would have to leave the UMC out of conscience. At the same time, those who are working toward full inclusion face a similar dilemma. They view the more restrictive language as being out of step with God's plan for an open, welcome, loving church.

I came to the UMC as an adult in 1980. When my wife and I were discussing whether of not we could be United Methodists, we prayed about our decision and we read books on Methodism. One of the books I read was *Beliefs of a United Methodist Christian*, by Bishop Emerson Colaw. One of the ideas that attracted me was that the UMC offered a broad tent: there are lots of ways to live out our Christian faith, and all United Methodists do not have to think and act alike on all issues. I have never agreed with everything that is in the *Book of Discipline*. I agree with the majority of it and I have not yet allowed those pieces I disagree with to cause me to seriously consider leaving the UMC. As long as I can live out my Christian faith within the UMC, I will continue to do so.

So, my advice would be to consider whether the differences that exist are important enough to make it impossible for you to continue to live out your Christian faith within the UMC. If one concludes that she or he is no longer in good conscience able to remain within the fold of the UMC, then I believe that person should count the cost that must be paid for speaking up and speaking out. The cost varies in many ways. A person early in her career has different obstacles to overcome than one who is late in her career. An Elder who would potentially be giving up guaranteed appointments would pay a different cost than a Deacon who has no guarantee and who has had to find her or his appointment already. A Licensed Local Pastor who serves at the pleasure of the Bishop and is credentialed only as long as he or she is under appointment is in an entirely different position. Church staff members who find themselves in opposition to a pastor or PPRC that believes differently could have their positions terminated. Each person must weigh what they can and cannot live with. In doing so, he or she must choose if, when, and how to speak out. Speaking out, or holding one's tongue, carries a cost. Before making any decisions about stepping out of the denomination, pray about it, discuss it with your spouse if you have one, and with those to whom you turn for advice and counsel. Staying or leaving is a major decision; don't make it in a hurry or under pressure from another. And remember, God is still God, whatever we decide.

QUESTION 8: *What do you think will be the long-term effect of the Traditional Plan on the membership of the United Methodist church?*

It is hard to gauge the long-term effect at this point. Within the US there is more and more openness to the rights and inclusion of LGBTQ persons in many areas of our society. One of the fears of those who are more progressive is that younger people will refuse to become a part of a church that is exclusive. There are some signs that this may be well-founded. Some of the UM

Seminaries are apparently reporting that young folks who are looking at seminaries are not considering UM schools because of the perception of not being open to all. I believe it is too early to tell if this will become a trend that will affect our churches in years to come or not. Another potential unintended consequence of the passage of the Traditional Plan is that organizations that are related to the UMC such as hospitals, colleges, or other entities could step back and re-evaluate whether they are willing to continue to be affiliated with the UMC or to carry the Methodist name.

As far as attendance in our local churches, I do believe that it will be a mixed bag for a while. Some folks will withdraw their membership and move on to other more open churches. At the same time, for persons who lean traditional in their beliefs, the adoption of the Traditional Plan may keep them from stepping out of the UMC now. This vote will not resolve the divide within our church. The same issues that were on the table in St. Louis will most certainly be up for debate and discussion again in Minneapolis, MN at General Conference 2020. About a month before the Special General Conference, I did have a conversation with a pastor of a rural two-point charge. I asked if there was a lot of concern in her churches over the upcoming session in St. Louis. The pastor's response to me was that the vote would have little effect on her local churches. They were going to continue loving God and loving those in their community regardless of what was decided in St. Louis. They were not overly anxious about their future. If all churches would focus on their mission and ministry as those two churches plan to do, there still might be hope to be united as we move forward. I do believe that we have much more that unites us than divides us.

Question 9: *What would you say to a congregation which is exploring leaving the United Methodist fold?*

It is a major decision to pull a church out of the United Methodist Church, or any denomination for that matter. It is a choice that should "not be entered into unadvisedly, but reverently, discreetly, and in the fear of God."[4] First, I would ask "Are your differences with the denomination irreconcilable?" There are reasons that churches are United Methodist and why individuals are as well. There are churches in southeastern Ohio that trace their roots back to Francis Asbury and the earliest of the Circuit Riders. That is a lot of DNA to walk away from. Many UM's are "Cradle Methodists." They were born into the church, baptized, raised to trust God and live out their faith in this tradition. That is a lot to give up. Is leaving the UMC really something that your entire church is in favor of doing? Rarely does a church go out on its own and retain everyone through that transition. Are you willing to lose those who disagree with that decision? Once people walk away from the denomination, individually or as a church, it can be very difficult for them to return, even if they realize that they were mistaken. Being a part of the UMC means that each church participates in making disciples across the world. From Africa to Cambodia to Russia to Minneapolis to the Philippines, we all have a hand in that discipleship through our UMC connection.

Churches that are used to having their pastor appointed by the bishop and cabinet are likely to find the independent search process to be daunting. Does your congregation have the resources to afford the ministry that you need in your setting? Many small-membership churches cannot afford the cost of quality pastoral leadership apart from their current charge arrangement. I have known of churches in other denominations that operate on a "call" system that have gone for extended periods of time without being able to find pastoral leadership. Is your church prepared to do that if an appropriate leader cannot be found? Each church is unique and will have circumstances that require special care to address. Don't make any decisions hurriedly, but make them prayerfully and be open to all voices, not just a few.

QUESTION 10: *What practices and spiritual disciplines should small groups and individuals participate in as they seek to discern a way forward?*

There are no practices or spiritual disciplines that work for everyone. Different people respond to a variety of practices and spiritual disciplines in many diverse ways. Obviously, prayers for discernment are a necessity. As we prepared for the Conference in St. Louis, my wife and I fasted for 24 hours each week from June of 2018 until February of 2019. We were seeking God's guidance as we went into this setting. While my wife and I did not agree on everything, we felt it was important to try to be open to God's leading in our lives. Reading the scriptures in their entirety is also helpful, I believe. What are the major tenets of the faith? Is the UMC as a whole and my local church in particular, trying to live out those tenets?

John Wesley also provided a very helpful practice for discernment, known as the Quadrilateral. The *Book of Discipline* states it this way: "While we acknowledge the primacy of Scripture in theological reflection, our attempts to grasp its meaning always involve tradition, experience, and reason. Like Scripture, these may become creative vehicles of the Holy Spirit as they function within the Church. They quicken our faith, open our eyes to the wonder of God's love, and clarify our understanding."[5] In using the quadrilateral, we are seeking to know the word of God more fully. We are attempting to learn what the scripture meant to the first persons who heard or read it, and to apply it to our 21st century lives. The Bible is the living word of God, and it continually surprises me as I read and read again, the old familiar words.

My God be with you and your church, as you respond in faith to God's leading in your life.

My dear brothers and sisters, take note of
this: Everyone should be quick to listen,
slow to speak and slow to become
angry, because human anger does not
produce the righteousness that God
desires.

James 1:19-20

TWO

What Would Jesus Hear?

BY BILL KEMP

T hroughout the gospels, we see Jesus going to have dinner in the homes of the outcast members of society. My favorite mention of this is at the beginning of the fifteenth chapter of Luke. The religious leaders accuse Jesus of welcoming sinners and eating with them (verse 2). Jesus responds to this criticism with a series of stories in which someone demonstrates an unusual concern for an item or person who others might consider to be not worth searching for. So, we have a lost sheep (verses 3-7), a lost coin (verses 8-10), and a lost son (verses 11-32). The movement from a shared animal to personal property to a family member, demonstrates that Jesus is upping the stakes with each story. When we get to the familiar prodigal son, we know that our heavenly father searches for us and considers each individual worth his attention. None of us are disposable.

Obviously, reconciling the lost members of his society with the mainstream was a key aspect of Jesus' ministry. Why else would he eat with the outcast? Why else would he go out of his way to aggravate the religious and political leaders of each town he visited? If Jesus came this week to be the guest preacher at your church, who would get him for lunch and why? Now let me ask one further question: why did Jesus' preference for dining with the marginalized upset everyone's expectations?

The simple answer to the first question is that Jesus was compassionate towards everyone, equally. This has been the "go to" answer for the United Methodist Church: "*We have Open Doors, Open Minds, Open Hearts*" and we want everyone to feel welcomed in our church. My calling this the simple answer, however, implies that we can't make it a resting place; we need to go further. What if Jesus ate with sinners because he knew that the people society rejected were easy to win over? Jesus was founding a movement. He was on a mission. He had church pews to fill.

I know that the above seems crass. I'm not asking my questions because I want you to conclude that Jesus only wanted to be popular. I'm saying this so you will listen with fresh ears to what is being said today in the United Methodist Church in Jesus' name. We want to welcome everyone because we want to be popular. And we, too, want to grow. We have church pews to fill. We have an institution to support and our mission share (apportionments) to pay.

I think this is the number one reason for the divide in our church today: the year 2019 comes at the end of a fifty-year decline in church membership and attendance. Many in church leadership have become desperate.

We seek for an answer and we have found two:

Answer A: Some people, let's call them *traditionalists*, believe the United Methodist Church is in decline because we have strayed from the Bible. We have stopped speaking about sin. Because we welcome sinners without asking them to stop sinning, we have dumbed down the gospel. Traditionalists point to the large non-denominational "box" churches that grow like weeds in every American suburb and ask "Why are the congregations with a conservative message growing, while mainstream denominations like the Episcopalians, Presbyterians, and recently, the Methodists, dying? If you want to make the UMC popular again, then go back to the kind of evangelism that calls homosexuality a sin."

Answer B: Others, let's call them *progressives*, point instead to the way all of America's traditional institutions are being devalued. Blame it on Watergate, or the 2008 Mortgage crisis, or the fall of Bill Cosby, we no longer trust those whom our parents trusted. When church leaders say, "Homosexuality is a sin," those with LGBTQ friends and family say, "What do they know?" Further, progressives see a great untapped mission field among those who feel marginalized, whether that sense of being an outcast comes from their immigration status, their poverty, or their gender fluidity. These people are tired of being called losers. They need a church that welcomes them as they are, without any expectation that they change. Yes, progressives, too, want the church to be popular again.

It's not really important whether you choose Answer A or Answer B. In fact, if you are leading a small group on this topic, you should avoid discussing which answer is the right one. The question is, can you hear the other answer? Can you listen to those who are staking their hopes for the church on an answer which is different from yours?

I would say to both Progressives and Traditionalists that they are being overly optimistic about their answer. Church popularity rises and falls. There are eras when the pews are full and times when being faithful is a lonely business. Throughout our 2000-year history, popularity hasn't always brought wisdom to the Church. Consider the Crusades.

It is important to hear that both progressives and traditionalists can be evangelical and motivated by an authentic desire to share the good news of Jesus Christ. Both sides also alienate newcomers by seeming to shift their values to build their membership. People know when we are being genuine. How? They experience us listening to them.

What Jesus Was Doing

Let me stretch you. What if the incarnation of the Holy God into our world was as an intentional listener? Jesus went into the homes of sinners, not so he could continue his preaching at them, but so he could listen to them. They accepted him into their hearts because he heard them. God is omniscient and didn't need to send Jesus to know us better. Instead, Jesus came to share our burdens and to feel firsthand the difficulties of the human condition. The incarnation was an act of divine empathy.

*If Jesus came and only had an hour to spend in your congregation, with whom would he go into a quiet place, and spend that hour listening to?

*If Jesus were to come to your community -- Stop! Don't

imagine who you wish he would preach at. No. But, who would he take the time to listen to?

The Holy Scriptures begin with Spirit of God brooding over the face of this deep and yet unformed creation. Before there was a pronouncement or a blueprint or a way forward, there was an unfathomable listening. Before there was jot or tittle or line set out to be the canon of scripture, there was listening.

What should we learn from this?

- Whenever we lack the patience to listen, we also lack the wisdom to be godly.
- Not only is God good all the time, God listens all the time.
- Simply quoting a few scriptures, having an authority preach, or passing a church policy, doesn't end the need for holy conversation.
- Other?

Jesus is listening to the United Methodist Church. What we read in the gospels should lead us to expect listening to occur in one-to-one and small group encounters. Large groups are the expected venues for official pronouncements and human legislation. But God-fearing hearts are addressed in a more personal fashion. Jesus engaged his little group of twelve disciples in a much more intense way than he did the crowds gathered on the hillsides. He listened to them. He used open dialogue to nurture them into being his representatives.

* When Jesus listens to your local church, what does he hear today?

(If you are doing this as a group study, each participant

should have the time to write several words or a short line. These should then be shared without comment or response from the others. Follow this with a time of simple, meditative, and/or silent prayer.)[1]

Being Intentional

To the casual observer, it would seem that we United Methodists are divided over the existence of homosexual clergy and the practice, now legal in most states, of marrying same-sex couples. If we could just come up with some rules for these things, and get everyone to follow them, then we could put the whole mess behind us. But the casual observer is not the listening participant. If you choose to listen, then you will hear a more nuanced account.

United Methodists want to live the Christian life. It is important to us that we encourage those things that are compatible with Christian teaching and condemn whatever violates Christian teaching. Today, discussions focus on where certain sexual practices, such as homosexuality, lie on the compatible-incompatible continuum. No one is arguing that certain sexual practices, such as pedophilia, are incompatible with Christian teaching. On the other hand, consensual sex between a man and a woman who are married to each other is definitely a part of the Christian lifestyle. We condemn sex which is violent or when the power balance is wrong, as between an adult and a child. We condone sex within marriage, where intimacy supports a life-long partnership (see Chapter 8, "What's Love Got to Do with It?"). Does anyone stand outside this consensus?

How then can we know the boundaries of this Christian lifestyle? I contend that listening to scripture, scientific reason, current culture, and church history (some of which we are not proud of), should come before our speaking any word on this subject. There are three common tactics that short-circuit this needed discussion:

- **The slippery slope argument** - Some people worry that if we fail to take a firm stand against homosexuality, then in a few years there will be polygamous trios wanting to be married together. What's next after that? Bestiality? Loss of support for the institution of marriage altogether? This argument displays a cynical distrust of the next generation. Each day we must seek the best wisdom for the current ethical dilemma.

- **Lumping it altogether** - "They are all the same," a church member says. Many people believe, without any research on this, that homosexuals are more prone than heterosexuals to pedophilia and less likely to develop long-term monogamous relationships. The very term LGBTQ (Lesbian, Gay, Bisexual, Transgendered, or otherwise Questioning/Queer) implies a variety of individual circumstances. It is likely that different components of this issue belong in differing places on the "compatible-incompatible with Christian teaching" continuum.

- **We don't have time to talk about it** - We all have enough time to do the things we value. The church has enough time to consider carefully the issues that deal with its core values (see Chapter 4, "What Would John Wesley

Think?"). Christians have plenty of time, perhaps an eternity, to listen to individuals and consider their circumstances as they relate to serious ethical choices.

* If you are studying this book in a group, you may want to pause and decide how you will respond when a group member uses one of the above tactics to short- circuit needed discussion.

The current debate in the United Methodist Church tends to focus on homosexuality. There are similar conversations relating to gender identity that deserve separate attention. What support should the church provide to people who do not relate to the gender they were assigned at birth? Because we feel safe with the traditional "binary" (you are what the doc told your parents you were) ways of speaking about gender, these conversations may make us feel uncomfortable. If we are pursuing the Christian lifestyle, and potentially defining it for others, shouldn't we go beyond our comfort zone?

PERHAPS SOME GROUND RULES MAY HELP:

1. We don't have to speak about or understand any specific sexual act. We do have to listen to the stories of people who find themselves in loving relationships that we don't understand.
2. We don't have to talk about the complications of cross-dressing, the different gender reassignment options, or even wrap our heads around the concept of gender fluidity. We do have to be willing to listen

when legitimate research discredits our comfortable
assumptions.

3. We should never assume that current secular culture
   speaks for God. People today are as sinful and short-
   sighted as any previous generation. We do have to
   hear, however, what the best minds and spiritual
   hearts of our era are saying.

4. What ground rules do you need to engage in this
   conversation?

I would ask you to listen for where the wind of God's spirit
is moving. Where is church vitality being recovered? Where is
Jesus Christ finding new disciples?

Three More Rules

The problem is that once we start to listen, we may soon find
ourselves drawn into a confusing place where we no longer
know which end is up. People remain casual observers of life
because it is convenient. Who wants to have their comfortable,
hand-me-down conclusions upset? Still, the Holy Spirit urges us
to remain engaged. The scriptures are full of stories of faithful
people who set out into the unknown, leaving their comfort
zone behind.

I have found three rules that keep me oriented in ethical
discussions. I'm often confused about the facts, but the guiding
principles of the search for truth are always true. These three
rules seem universal. They can be found in the spiritual writings
of many traditions. There are many scriptures that support these

rules, but I like to use Jesus' story of the Good Samaritan. They are:

1) Always be compassionate
2) Awareness beats ignorance
3) The ends never justify the means

Consider now, the familiar story of the Good Samaritan - Luke 10:30-37

Always be Compassionate means in every situation, do the thing that shows authentic love for the other person. It can be expressed as the Golden Rule, that we should do unto others as we would hope they would do for us (Matthew 7:12). In the story of the Good Samaritan it is seen in the Samaritan turning aside to help a stranger who has been beaten on the road from Jerusalem to Jericho. Jesus makes a point of saying how this act involved the Samaritan's compassion towards a person who was different and unknown.

* How does your church encourage it members to take risks in personal acts of compassion?

Awareness beats Ignorance means that the Samaritan crosses the road to investigate the nature of the man's injuries. It means we take time to hear the stories of those whose experience is different from our own.

* When have you gone further than you wanted to in order to understand a situation or another person's problem?

The Ends never Justify the Means involves always following an honorable, appropriate, and healthy process when you are making decisions involving other people. For the lawyer and the scribe in Jesus' story, walking by the man beaten beside the road was justified by the all-important end of making it to the temple in time for worship. Often in politics, dirty tricks are used to achieve some end result. Saying the ends never justify the means is to say that we are committed to behaving in the right way, even if it prevents us from meeting whatever goal we have set for ourselves.

* DOES THE END OF MAKING THE CHURCH GROW JUSTIFY A MEANS that might leave some people out of the church?

THIS FINAL QUESTION TAKES US BACK TO THE FIRST QUESTION, "WHY does Jesus have dinner in the homes of the most outcast members of his society?"

THREE

The Art of Listening

BY DARRELL COATES

Historically, the great internal conflicts within the Methodist people, as well as the actual occasions of church schism, have happened when our nation has been politically fragmented. The diversity we see today in worship, religious identity, and theological understanding between local United Methodist Churches mirrors the mobility and multicultural nature of our modern world, as well as the increasing pluralism of American life. Too often, we respond to cultural diversity in unhealthy ways. We separate into opposing teams. Our discussions become polarized. The 2019 Special General Conference meeting in St Louis has to be viewed against this backdrop. The specific issue at hand involves the acceptance of LGBTQ persons and the church's changing views on human sexuality. The actual legislation passed is one part of the picture. The bigger picture, however, involves how we continue these discussions within the local church.

Will we listen to each other?

Whether we hear them or not, the following discussions are already taking place in your congregation:

1) Will our denomination's recent reaffirmation of the doctrine that "homosexuality is incompatible with Christian teaching" affect what we personally believe? Does it change the way we relate to our fellow members, family, and friends, who identify as LGBTQ?

2) What will we expect our Christian education staff and youth leaders to teach about human sexuality? Will we consider certain teachings as grounds for dismissal? What do we wish our pastor would do or say about these issues?

3) Should we on the church's website, Facebook page, or some other public location, publish a statement announcing our congregation's stance regarding human sexuality?

* Pause now to note which of the above conversations you have overheard or participated in. If you are studying this book with a group, be careful not to digress into a debate about the issues. The focus of this chapter is on whether or not people feel safe to talk, and if they feel heard. What additional questions or concerns are being raised?

Are We Listening?

Compounding our inherent difficulties with listening to each other is the fact that LGBTQ issues aren't just surface or topical issues. The deeper issues driving our current conflict are **relational** (i.e., How do I relate to you when you are different from me?) and **identity** issues (i.e., How do I see myself and how do I see you?). Until we address these deeper issues, we are simply affixing a Band-Aid. Jesus was accused of many things, but impatience wasn't one of them. When we fail to listen fully, we are being impatient, and that always exacts a cost. Even now, following the 2019 Special General Conference, we must acknowledge that taking a vote hasn't ended our need for discussion. We need to rebuild relationships. We need to understand how personal identity shapes what a person believes. Until we learn effective communication, the church will continue to fragment.

One of the most precious gifts we can give another person is listening. Are we willing to give this gift to each person we meet within the United Methodist Church? We can't offer that gift if the other person doesn't feel safe talking to us. We must treat all conversations regarding human sexuality with a certain level of confidentiality. Further, people never feel listened to when the verbal, non-verbal, or passive response we are making implies that we are judging them. Effective communication depends upon active, empathetic, and intentional listening.

Active Listening involves giving beneficial feedback to the speaker through both brief verbal responses and nonverbal clues, at the appropriate times throughout the conversation, so the speaker knows he is being heard. Active listeners avoid interrupting the speaker and limit their own comments to what is needed to understand the other person. The appropriate time to share what you have to say is after you fully understand what the other person means. Beneficial feedback often takes the form of "checking in," that is, saying phrases such as, "I understand that you are saying…" or, "let me see if I am hearing you right…" Many marriages could be saved if only we were in the habit of giving the other persons sufficient time to explain what they mean.

Empathetic Listening means demonstrating to the speakers that you understand their feelings and affirm their right to have these emotions. Non-empathetic listeners often discount, or seek to diminish, the feelings that other people are experiencing. Whereas, empathetic listeners give appropriate encouragement, saying, "Tell me more about how that made you feel," and, "I can understand. If I had the same experience, I might feel the same way."

Consider the following example:

Speaker – *"When I tell people in this church that I believe marriage is just between a man and a woman, I feel judged."*

Inactive Listener - *"Wait a minute! I've never judged you."*

Un-empathetic Listener - *"You shouldn't feel that way. You need to develop a thicker skin."*

Intentional Listening is predicated on a certain amount of trust. We have to believe that if we actively and empathetically listen, our turn will come. When it is our turn to speak, we hope that we will be heard with the same grace we have shown to others by our listening. Good listeners are often pleasantly surprised to discover that when their turn to speak finally comes, what they have to say has been transformed and improved by what they have heard.

The Communication Process

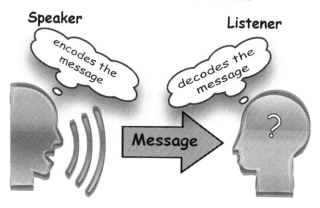

The Communication Process

As I said before, one of the most precious gifts we can give people is really listening to them. Many of us, especially those of us in church leadership, assume that effective communication depends upon our choosing the right words and being able to get our point across. We hear the familiar adage that communication is a two-way street, and think, "Well, maybe it's 50-50." To really become an effective communicator, however, we need to intentionally shift to 90% listening and 10% speaking. This is because hearing and understanding what another person is saying is never as easy as we think. The listening elements of the communication process are many times more complex than the speaking elements.

As we transmit a message, we encode it with a variety of non-verbal signals such as eye contact, facial expression, voice inflection, body posturing and hand gestures. The recipient of the message must decode the transmitted message by taking into account both words and gestures, content and affect. In other words, the person hearing the message must also **interpret** it.

Every time we speak, our message is encoded first into words, which may have a different meaning or come with certain "baggage" for the listener. Then, subconsciously aware that these words may be ambiguous, we overlay our message with a wide range of nonverbal signals. This body language can itself be misunderstood or lead to a break in communication. When we feel deeply about what is being said, our attention shifts from the literal words to the nonverbal aspects of the exchange. With emotionally charged issues, such as gender identity and whom a person is allowed to love, it is reasonable to expect a greater percent of the communication process to happen nonverbally. How much? Dr. Albert Mehrabian has observed that emotionally charged topics are typically conveyed thusly: 7% verbally, 38% vocally, and 55% through body posture and physical gestures. [1]

* Reflect upon or discuss the following:

- When have you failed to hear someone because the non-verbal layer laid on top of the words frightened or confused you?
- How do you prefer to address sensitive subjects? Are you more comfortable speaking directly to the person (where words and body language are combined), or over the phone (where the nonverbal layer is limited vocal tone and pauses), or by written communication (texts, email, letters, etc.)?

- Remember the last time you went to a coworker, boss, or doctor with a problem. Did they demonstrate empathy as they listened to you?

It is never enough to focus on only the content of a message. To truly hear other people, we must also note their gestures, tone, facial expression, etc., and interpret the emotional component of their message. This requires skill, practice, and empathy.

Filter Bubbles

Our past wedges itself like a filter between us and those with whom we are communicating. Every person lives in a bubble formed by culture and experience. We hear what we have been conditioned to hear. In other words, we are isolated from those who are different from us and we each process the world through a variety of filters. Effective communicators seek to understand and compensate for their own filter bubble.[2]

Our filters are so much a part of our own identity that we are unaware of the blind spots they create in our understanding of others. In subtle and unconscious ways, they influence what we perceive. They shape the way we interpret events, establish priorities, and pass judgment on others. Being aware of these filters and how they block our ears is an important first step toward effective listening.

Think of the experiences and influences that have made you the unique person you are. Those experiences provide us with the lenses we use to interpret the world. There are generational lenses. For example, persons who came of age during the

Depression view luxuries very differently from those who have never been in need. Millennials, that is, those who came of age near the year 2000, have a natural acceptance of technology, viewing it as a given, neither good nor bad. There are economic lenses. Those who grew up in poverty often filter their world through what is needed right now. Middle-class people weigh the future more heavily in their perceptions. The wealthy filter their experience through the past. There are also regional filter bubbles, separating what urban, rural, and suburban people assume to be common sense. Formative childhood memories involving race, ethnicity, sexual orientation, and immigration status, obviously shape our filter bubble.

* REFLECT ON AND DISCUSS THE ABOVE PARAGRAPH. IT IS FULL OF broad generalizations. When you found yourself objecting to a stereotype, was it because your own experience and the factors that shaped your personal filter bubble are unique to you?

* CONSIDER THE OPENING TO JESUS' SERMON ON THE MOUNT (Matthew 5:3-12). How would a person bringing each of the following stereotypical filter bubbles hear Jesus' words?

1) A holocaust survivor?

2) An adult who was bullied in high school because his outward appearance and mannerisms did not match his gender.

3) A person who now manages a successful business that was begun by his hardworking parents.

• • •

* Now, REFLECT UPON OR DISCUSS HOW THE POLITICAL polarization of our country may be exacerbated by various filter bubbles. It has been noted that Fox News intentionally cultivates an audience with one filter bubble and MSNBC the opposite filter bubble. Do you feel that politicians are opportunistically accentuating the effect of our prejudices and filter bubbles?

Confirmation Bias

Filter Bubbles reinforce another barrier to communication known as Confirmation Bias. Think of the last time you had to make a big purchase with only a limited amount of information. Say you buy a new car and for a while it performs beautifully and meets your expectations. You think, "Boy, I was smart to buy that car." This confirmation of your luck or wisdom leads you to be *biased* favorably towards the car in the future. The car may begin to function badly, but you will discount any negative experiences and focus on the events that *confirm* you made a good choice in picking this car. We want to think we know more than we know. We want to view ourselves as making mostly good choices. Confirmation Bias maintains this false optimism. It also can shield us from hearing the arguments that others are making against what we have already decided.

What if instead of purchasing a car, we are deciding which politician to vote for? In the past, we have decided for candidates from a certain party. Our filter bubble may have predisposed us to lean towards conservatives or towards more liberal candidates. Each time we make a decision in that same direction, our Confirmation Bias kicks in. We feel confident that we already know the right choice. We can discount the negative news stories, and pat ourselves on the back as each positive story confirms our bias. Incumbent politicians love confirmation bias.

But what if we are engaged in communicating about sensitive and personal situations? What if we are seeking to step outside our filter bubble and hear the scriptures in a new way? What if certain people in our congregation have made different life choices than ours and we want to understand their decisions? Can we hear them without discounting the places where their story reflects negatively on our decisions?

THIS IS WHAT THE PROPHET ISAIAH HEARS GOD SAYING:

Forget the former things;
do not dwell on the past.
See, I am doing a new thing!
Now it springs up; do you not perceive it?
I am making a way in the wilderness
and streams in the wasteland.

Isaiah 43:18-19

Feedback Loops

Learning to be an effective listener is a lifelong process. It requires you to discover and implement new tools for understanding. This chapter has provided only a handful of techniques. Key to becoming an active, empathetic, and intentional listener is providing beneficial feedback to the one who is speaking. Small group meetings within the church provide an excellent place to practice our listening skills. Try this at your next committee meeting: when someone proposes an idea you don't care for, stop and think how you might provide beneficial feedback. You might say, *"It seems to me you are saying..."* and rephrase the idea in your own words. Then check to see if you did hear it right. This going back and forth, giving the others as much time as they need to express and clarify their idea, adds feedback loops to our conversations. Feedback loops make even difficult discussions gentler and more productive.

You may be in a Bible study or prayer meeting. Another participant brings up a sensitive issue. He may be making himself vulnerable, trusting the group with a place where brokenness or doubt is overshadowing his faith. As an active and intentional listener, you can encourage him with verbal and nonverbal feedback. You may say things like; *"That must be very upsetting..."*, *"You seem to be disappointed..."* or *"It sounds like you're feeling some anger..."* Don't be afraid to get it wrong. The speaker will correct you and appreciate that you cared enough to try and acknowledge his feelings. In order for the speaker to feel that he has been genuinely heard, listeners must be willing to take risks and give authentic feedback.

This book has been developed to encourage small group meetings and healing discussions in the United Methodist Church around the LBGTQ issue. A positive outcome is not dependent upon gathering more information, or taking another vote, or finding an equitable way to separate into different camps. We will not get past our confirmation bias and filter bubbles without effective communication, complete with intentional, beneficial feedback loops.

You can tell that we are good United Methodist penguins because our hearts are strangely warmed, we desire to transform the world, and we regularly flock together in holy conferences.

Do not conform to the pattern of this world, but be transformed by the renewing of your mind. Then you will be able to test and approve what God's will is—his good, pleasing and perfect will.

- Romans 12:2

FOUR

What Would John Wesley Think?

BY BILL KEMP

To make a bird, you need three things; feathers, a set of wings, and the ability to lay an egg. To make a Methodist, that is, a Christian within the Wesleyan tradition, you need three things: 1) a personal faith that is going on to perfection, 2) a desire to organize so as to transform the world, and 3) a set of rules that connect us with other Methodists, as we gather in congregations, districts, annual conferences, and every four years, in general conferences. And yes, it must be said, that when General Conference meets to legislate the rules that govern it all, it often lays an egg.

Imperfect as they appear in everyday church life, these are our core values. They go back to John Wesley, who in the mid-1700s inadvertently organized a movement that split off from the Church of England. Where the old church valued the outward and formal aspects of congregational life, the new Wesleyan movement emphasized personal piety and the sanctification (the lifelong spiritual formation), of every believer.

Where the old church managed a centuries-old parish structure that provided clergy, worship services, and church buildings to the English people in a very orderly fashion, the Wesleyan revival organized itself to utilize small groups, society meetings, and circuit riders. It was a movement designed to cross barriers and evangelize new people. The Church of England maintained a fixed hierarchy with little input from laity. Ordained clergy were tenured into this top-down organization. Our church grew out of the "Holiness Club" that John and Charles Wesley attended while students at Oxford and which, from its earliest days, had a democratic spirit that valued the consensus and discernment of groups guided by prayer over the traditions established by men (gender specificity intended). These three values; an emphasis on personal piety, a missional spirit, and an intentional deference to the discernment of prayerful and diverse groups (sometimes known as holy conferencing) are baked into every page of our history.

I would argue that the above three values distinguish the denominations that care about John Wesley, and what he would think if he were alive today, from those denominations that aren't part of our immediate church family. These agreed-upon values, however, have *not* served to unite us. Over the last 240 years, the Methodist people have often been divided, usually with members of each opposing camp claiming they are the real keepers of John Wesley's heritage. For example, the predecessors of the United Brethren Church thought of themselves as children of Wesley, but for various reasons, including the use of the German language during worship, weren't included in the main body of the Methodist Church. On the other hand, the divisions were sometimes amicable and practical, extending the outreach of the Wesleyan movement.

John Wesley himself, however, hated the infighting that so often happens within church bodies. He was reluctant to separate Methodism from the Church of England, even though his movement was constantly under attack and its clergy members forbidden to preach in its pulpits. He lived with a paradox. He believed the Holy Spirit to be a great unifier and that all Christians, no matter where they worshiped, shared an equal access to God's grace. Yet, whenever he followed the leadings of the Holy Spirit, he found himself in controversy. He valued fellowship and constantly sought to invite new people into the fold, not wishing any theological quibble or social norm to be a barrier. He said, "Though we can't think alike, may we not love alike?" (Wesley's Sermons, "Catholic Spirit"). But throughout his long career, he trusted in reason, tradition, and church law, to settle controversial issues and establish boundaries around Methodist membership.

Even before Methodism separated from the Church of England, the debate between slave-holders and abolitionists began to separate Christian from Christian, denomination from denomination. Quakers and Mennonites decided that slavery was incompatible with Christian teaching. Most other denominations decided not to decide. In the United States, however, social and political realities made it impossible, and perhaps immoral, for the church to remain neutral. American Methodism divided into Northern and Southern churches. The mid-1800s also witnessed the formation of racially segregated denominations within the Wesleyan fold. If we were able to time-travel and witness those contentious church gatherings, we might note some similarities to our current moment. Back then, both sides quoted scripture and spoke of their heartfelt convictions. The underlying issue concerned whether you could separate an individual's standing in society from his role within the church. Can an individual be both a fellow Christian and a slave? Can an LGBTQ individual be accepted as a full and productive member of society, and yet denied a leadership role within the United Methodist Church?

Shortly after the merger that formed the United Methodist denomination in 1968, a series of cultural pressures which were unrelated to the merger began to polarize our newly united church. A perfect storm emerged. Each of the three Wesleyan values lent themselves, seemingly equally, to opposite sides of the LGBTQ inclusion question. We cannot resurrect John Wesley and ask him to solve our current dilemma. He had enough heartbreak with the controversies of his day. We can, however, seek to understand how each of the core Wesleyan values informs our current discussion.

* Read each section below and pause. Take time to note, or discuss if you are in a group, how well you understand the opposing position to which others might arrive while following the same value.

Personal Faith

For John Wesley, the grace of God and our personal faith in God manifested itself in two ways; first, by the salvation of the believer, and second, by changes in the believer's outward behavior. This second grace, or sanctification, was a call to for each believer to become holier each day, in thought, word, and action. Methodists were methodical about going on to perfection in holiness. Our list of particular outward signs included: dressing modestly, avoiding profanity, attending additional church gatherings (particularly Wednesday and Sunday evening prayer meetings), fasting regularly, and abstaining from work on the Sabbath, as well as from alcohol, tobacco, gambling, quarreling, and extra-marital sex. Even before the LGBTQ debate came to the fore, United Methodists were divided about how about important particular outward acts of holiness were to personal faith. When was the last time you heard a sermon about modest dress or fasting? Although listing undesirable behaviors fits with Wesley's Enlightenment-era world view, it feels at odds with today's understanding of personal faith.

The General Rules, which are a part of our United Methodist Discipline, adds to the above list such items as extravagance, shirking duties and taxes, borrowing without intent to repay, singing profane songs and/or reading trashy books, etc. One of the ways that our church culture has adjusted to changes in modern attitudes about a holiness list, is to ask only our clergy persons to adhere to the General Rules. This was certainly not John Wesley's intent. In 1984, the United Methodist Church added to its Discipline a prohibition against practicing homosexuals from becoming clergy, reasoning that since same-sex marriage was illegal at the time, all practicing homosexuals were engaging in extra-marital sex.

* DO YOU FEEL THAT THE LEGALIZATION OF SAME-SEX MARRIAGE IN many states has changed the list of acceptable behaviors for our clergy persons?

The other response to our postmodern shift away from asso-
ciating personal faith with a list of changed behaviors is to focus
our call to perfection on making our relationships more loving.
Personal faith leads us to be more authentic and loving in our
dealings with those around us. Further, the behaviors we seek to
change are those that harm other people. The General Rules
begin with an encouragement to *first, do no harm*. They continue
with an encouragement to *do all the good that we can*.[1] United
Methodists agree that personal faith should lead every Christian
to be committed to acts of compassion and justice. We disagree,
however, on the degree to which LBGTQ concerns are legitimate
justice issues.

* WHEN MATTERS OF PERSONAL FAITH AND INDIVIDUAL SIN ARE
preached or taught in your church, should the emphasis be
upon turning away from certain practices, or upon our personal
relationship with God?

PASTORS ARE OFTEN ASKED TO PROVIDE A RULING ABOUT WHETHER A
particular act was a sin or not. This question implies a certain
list of bad behaviors that is external to the individual. What if
we turn the question around and ask, "Do you feel this behavior
interferes with your relationship with God?"

* HOW DO YOU RESPOND TO INDIVIDUALS WHO FEEL THAT BEING
LGBTQ doesn't violate their personal conscience? Is it possible
to be a "holiness church" but allow for different lists of sins?

Collaborative Mission

The Anglican communion that Methodism departed from had little interest in evangelism beyond the church walls. By way of contrast, John Wesley said, "The world is my parish." He preached in the open air to coal miners, who because of the work week were cut off from church life. It has been estimated that over a million people were converted during Wesley's lifetime as a direct result of the Methodist movement. We accept people where they are and love them into becoming faithful disciples of Jesus Christ. Methodist mission work and evangelism found particularly fertile ground in the American colonies where circuit riders offered the sacraments and marriage ceremonies to people cut off from more static institutions.

This emphasis upon mission, however, has long been plagued by competing understandings about human nature and how the world is to be transformed. Many United Methodists say that we transform the world by supporting social justice, by meeting the needs of hurting people, and by lovingly accepting those who differ from us. This end of the continuum has a certain optimism about human history. God's plan for the church is to form people into effective disciples, with everyone working together to make the world a better place. Jesus enables us to love, and this doesn't mean forcing our religious and morals down everyone's throat.

Other United Methodists, however, fear that world is so fallen into sin, that we can only transform it by converting a majority to Christianity. As previously noted, Wesleyan people believe that salvation leads to a more holy lifestyle. When Christian principles are widespread, the world becomes a better place. This view of missions has a certain pessimism about human nature. In the extreme, it says, "The world is going to hell in a hand-basket and our mission is to rescue those we can before Jesus returns."

While all United Methodists value mission and evangelism, we differ in our worldview. Some of us have a progressive optimism. We feel that humanity is gradually learning what it means to be human. As one hymn says, *Time makes ancient good uncouth"* (*Once to Every Man and Nation* by James Russell Lowell). When it comes to the LGBTQ issues, those with a progressive worldview expect to see the church adopting a more science-based and healthy understanding of human sexuality. Progressives also feel that church teachings and leadership expectations must be constantly modified to reflect best practices and current understandings about ethics and morality.

Everything about that last paragraph offends those with a more traditional view of human depravity. When Methodism first took hold in the United States, our mission was simply to spread scriptural holiness across the land. Why has it changed today? Those with a more pessimistic view of current society point to the opioid epidemic, the rise in violent conflicts abroad, and this generation's acceptance or abortion as an option, and ask why the church isn't speaking more fervently about sin. Our mission, as they see it, is to evangelize those foreign countries and those pockets within our society that are willing to accept Jesus as Lord and guide them into a holier lifestyle.

The quickest way to create an argument between progressive and traditionalist thinkers is to use the word *postmodern*. Post-modernism is the widely-accepted sociological term for the shift in popular culture that occurred after the modern era (from the

Renaissance through the first World War). John Wesley was fully embedded in the modern era, and his writings display the comforting certainty he found in reason, science, and institutions, such as the British monarchy. Those nostalgic for the modern era play bridge, because a spade is always a spade, and the fixed hierarchy of ace, king and queen displays the God-ordained order of this world. But our current culture is more familiar with the random chaos of video games. Postmoderns lost their faith in institutions, including the church, with Watergate and the Vietnam War. Living after the Holocaust and being profoundly influenced by the ministry of Dr. Martin Luther King, many Christians today feel that the great work of our era is to provide justice for all and to make the church as inclusive as possible. Postmodern ethics and theology are also influenced by relativistic science, with its non-Newtonian understanding of the physical world. In a quantum universe where the time and value of each event varies according to the observer, what is truth? If the coming apocalypse is more likely to be fueled by climate change than the events described in the book of Revelation, why is the church so silent on contemporary issues? Perhaps the biggest beef traditional--minded people have with the postmodern culture is that people today can consider themselves spiritual without being religious. This means that our whole approach to evangelism and missions needs to shift away from the goal of making more church members.

Both progressive and traditional-minded people need to accept postmodern culture as a given. Postmodernism was not caused by Methodists failing to preach about sin. Taking prayer out of schools and deciding Roe v Wade did not cause American Christian culture to collapse. If past history is any indicator of future events, we are still at the beginning of the postmodern era and it is likely to continue for many generations. The United Methodist Church will either adapt its mission efforts and internal church culture or it will die the slow death of all irrelevant institutions. Unfortunately, there are politicians and popular preachers who speak about postmodernity with fear and loathing. They may be helping their own platforms by promising a way back to a more sensible and religious era, but they are not helping the United Methodist Church with their snake oil. What playing bridge taught me is that you should always play the hand you are dealt, not the hand you wish you had.

* REFLECT ON OR DISCUSS: IS ACCEPTING PEOPLE WITHOUT ASKING them to change their sexual practices a mistaken compromise with postmodernity?

WHAT WOULD JOHN WESLEY THINK ABOUT THE LGBTQ ISSUE? Wesley, like the Apostle Paul before him, had a passionate and expansive understanding of the love of Jesus Christ for all people, coupled with a pragmatic approach to making the church a better vessel for that evangelical message (see Chapter Seven). That said, Wesley's few tangential references to homosexuality display the prejudices of his day. He lived in a different era from ours; sociology and psychology were yet to be invented as fields of scientific study and Thomas Jefferson's thoughts on individual freedom would seem avant-garde to Wesley.[2] Frankly, he would be unable to follow our current debate, let alone speak authoritatively on it. Wesleys most lasting gift to our denomination, however, was his genius for organization. Unfortunately, our current debate may lead us to wonder if we at last come to the end of that institutional legacy.

Holy Conferencing

To be Methodist is to be methodical. John Wesley had a gift for solidifying religious concepts into practical rules and policies. Since 1784, our church structure has been defined and refined by a system of holy conferencing. Each year, Annual Conferences meet to develop the mission plan for their region and to certify ministerial candidates. Bishops conference with their cabinet and appoint clergy to their charges. Every four years, a General Conference gathers to perfect our rulebook, the *Book of Discipline*. On rare occasions, a special General Conference session may be called to deal with specific issues.

The whole process was developed during the Enlightenment period, when democracies began to unseat monarchies. American Methodism has always valued democracy and the expansion of those who were invited to the leadership table. We have inherited an episcopal hierarchy, with bishops and their cabinets (district superintendents and conference officers) meeting in closed-door sessions to appoint clergy and discern matters affecting local congregations. Regarding church law, structure, and general policy, however, we vote in open conference, with the right to vote given equally to laity and clergy. United Methodist Bishops may have a special teaching role and appear to speak for the church. But when United Methodists gather to decide doctrine and general policy, bishops have limited authority. In fact, the role that Bishops play in General Conference has been described as being on stage like potted plants.

This Wesleyan value for a democratic process of Holy Conferencing places the United Methodist Church mid-way in a continuum of ways for governing a church. Roman Catholics, Episcopalians, and most Orthodox churches are to our right, both in looking to a hierarchy of ordained leaders to make major decisions and in expecting each local congregation and its members to be obedient to their policies. To our left are the denominations who place more authority in the local church and its lay leadership. At the far left end of this continuum are the non-denominational congregations who may turn to an association of like-minded churches and pastors for guidance, but expect most of their decisions to be made locally.

At the special General Conference in Saint Louis, the Council of Bishops voiced their support for a "One Church Plan," and true to our Wesleyan value for Holy Conferencing, this plan was voted down. The Traditional Plan, which was adopted, was based on a belief that bishops and conference boards of ministry who act in violation of the Discipline are failing to uphold their promise to be obedient to the decisions of the majority meeting at General Conference.

Many oppose the Traditional Plan and continue to look for ways to overturn it. While affirming the role that Holy Conferencing plays in our church, they argue:

- Our Wesleyan values also lead us to respect individual conscience. A majority vote doesn't make a LGBTQ person a sinner. In the postmodern era, church doctrine and teaching can't be determined at a council or a conference. Having a line in the *Book of Discipline* doesn't make it Gospel truth.
- That ministry and mission is always done in context. Denying LGBTQ people ordination and the opportunity to be married within the United Methodist Church offends the very people with whom God is calling us to be in ministry.
- That LGBTQ issues are a matter of social justice. The Holy Spirit is calling the church to lead. If Holy Conferencing is done right, with an obedience to prayer and an open mind, we will see that the current situation is similar to the churches' previous concerns about slavery and women clergy.

On Christian Teaching

John Wesley, if resurrected today, might question our process for determining church teaching regarding LGBTQ issues. Wesley demonstrated a lifelong preference for rigorous academic study over popular opinion polls for making serious decisions. His method for theological reflection, dubbed the "Wesleyan Quadrilateral" by Albert C. Outler, rested equally upon scripture, tradition, reason, and experience. Further, Wesley believed that an unbroken sacred linkage existed to the apostles through the chain of ordination. The proper interpretation of scripture and church traditions has been handed down from generation to generation, from the time of Jesus to our own, through an apostolic succession of popes and bishops. From time to time, councils of ordained clergy persons may meet, as they did for the Council of Nicaea in 325 AD, and make formal statements about church teaching. Holy Conferencing prayerfully discerns the right channel of doctrine, so to speak, when the great river of apostolic succession is seriously divided.

I would argue that Wesley intended the Discipline, as well as the later Social Principles (1972), to guide the organizational structure of the church and to prioritize our mission to make disciples for the transformation of the world. I doubt he would appreciate the line *"The United Methodist Church does not condone the practice of homosexuality and considers this practice incompatible with Christian teaching,"* (Paragraph 161.g, 2016 *Book of Discipline*) being inserted in our Discipline/Social Principles as a way to cut off ongoing discussion, or to definitively say what United Methodists believe. Further, he would think it odd that when the Special General Conference met in Saint Louis in 2019, the action of the majority went against the recommendations of the Council of Bishops and the rigorous academic study work done by the Way Forward committee.

About Wilderness

In the wilderness you will experience Denial, Anger, Bargaining, Depression, and Acceptance.

Spiritual wilderness is a part of every major change in life. Transitions like marriage, military service, retirement, and the death of a spouse are marked by both a change in our personal identity and a change in our outward circumstance. No matter how well we prepare for the onset of these changes, our entry into the next season of life can be disorienting. Navigating wilderness is challenging.

From time to time, nations, corporations, local congregations, etc., find themselves in the midst of an unexpected transition.

There are certain predictable aspects to these wilderness experiences, whether we look at what the United States faced following 911, or what Eastman Kodak went through following the advent of digital photography, or the wilderness the Tree of Life Congregation is currently traveling through following the mass shooting in Pittsburgh. Unpleasant transitions involve a profound sense of loss. Travel in the Wilderness often visits the five stages of grief outlined by Dr. Elisabeth Kübler-Ross:

Denial, Anger, Bargaining, Depression, and Acceptance

FIVE

Thoughts on Wilderness

BY KATHY MOORE

The story of the Exodus stirs the soul when we contemplate the experience of a people living in slavery who were suddenly released into freedom. This happened, not because the slaveholders eventually saw the error of their ways, and not because the enslaved stood up for their rights and fought for freedom, but simply because God said, "I have seen my people in slavery, and I want them to be freed" (Exodus 6:6).

This empowering tale of liberation and justice helps us recognize God's Will through Justice. The "arc of the universe" bends towards the just and fair treatment of all people (Dr. Martin Luther King). It is an image we can carry within us to keep us strong in the face of injustice and oppression "in whatever forms they present themselves."

To remember the Exodus is to ponder the goodness of God in choosing to set a people free, and to celebrate the freedom of a nation. Yet the story continues on past the actual escape from slavery, telling of forty years of pilgrimage in the wilderness.

Fear and Focus

Exodus is a story of wilderness wanderings, and this is an apt metaphor to help us face the struggles individuals and communities face on our journeys as we follow the Way (Acts 9:1-2). These struggles don't necessarily confront us as injustice or oppression; rather, they occur because of the vicissitudes of this imperfect life, and our own personal challenges. Exodus speaks to us of our fear of the future, and our inability to see anything else when we are focused on that fear.

When I toured the Middle East in 2018, the bus took us south out of Jerusalem, down into the Great Rift Valley, with the Dead Sea to our left, and all the way around the Sinai Peninsula before turning west to Cairo. While in Israel, I kept gazing at the rocks and sand. The barren desert and rugged stone began at Qumran, extended to the desert fortress of Masada, and down to the gulf of Aqaba. Our guide said it was probably close to this area, near the southern end of the Jordan, or perhaps across the Dead Sea, that Jesus was in the wilderness during his fasting and temptations (Mark 1:12-13). It was hard to imagine Jesus living there forty days and nights, even if he was fasting. In the Sinai, we drove on to an area back off the road where a man had fashioned a replica of the tent Moses built to house the Ark of the Covenant. This seemed even farther from food and water, and I couldn't imagine the Israelites surviving here. We visited the rugged land near St. Catherine's Monastery, built on Mount Sinai, the location where Moses reputedly received the Ten Commandments. Even the cats seemed to be starving there. And this was the area the Israelites wandered for forty years?

I imagine those ancient people taking one look at this desolate area and thinking, "What in the world is Moses doing? He thinks we can survive here?" No wonder they began to dream of the leeks and melons of Egypt. I always used to think they were awfully quick to murmur and mutter about Moses, every time they were worried. Now I understand their apprehensions a bit better, having seen their wilderness. *What will we eat? What will we drink? We've had this manna stuff until it's coming out our noses.* Murmuring to the point that Moses cried, "What shall I do with these people?" (Numbers 11).

The Israelites murmured because they were scared, and Moses was frustrated because they hadn't learned to trust God. They still feared the future. They complained about the uncertainty of the journey. Every time they approached Moses with their concerns, he went to God in prayer. The answer he received for them related to their fears: You're afraid of the Egyptian army? God will take you through the water. You fear hunger? Try this Bread of Heaven, called Manna. You're longing for meat you left behind in Egypt and fear the poverty of the desert? Here are hordes of quail flying right into your camp. You're thirsty? God can call up water from a rock. And on it went. Forty years in the wilderness. Forty years of God calming their anxieties and supplying their needs.

Wilderness wanderings have a corrosive effect on us. We find ourselves unable to count on a hopeful future. If we face a personal issue of health or finances, of problems with children or with in-laws, of losing a job or losing in love, of a loss of faith or loss of loved ones—whatever our own personal wilderness, we can't quite trust that God is working in our lives for good. In fact, when I'm in my own personal wilderness, I find it hard to sympathize with other people and their problems.[1]

Being in the wilderness changes us. We learn compassion. We survive. Wilderness shapes our spirit to be more sensitive and tender toward others in whatever difficulties they face, even if their suffering doesn't much resemble our own.

But while I am suffering, I don't really want to hear about your suffering. If you tell me, I am most likely to turn the conversation around to talk about my own troubles. Sometimes you may even think I'm telling you my troubles in order to convince you that you aren't so bad off. Yeah, you should really feel sorry for me!

As we walk our individual faith journeys, we often come to realize the way our painful wilderness experiences may be necessary for our own growth. Just as the Israelites needed the wilderness in order to be prepared for the Promised Land, we need to work through the struggle or pain of our wanderings. We may have a crisis of faith not unlike the Children of Israel, and that experience may finally lead us to a deeper faith.

"Wilderness" is currently a leading topic in faith development, devotion and spiritual formation books, and most of them seem focused on individual faith. But the wanderings of the Children of Israel involved a community, and we are struggling within our own communities, congregations, and conferences.

In our denomination, we are experiencing wilderness wanderings, even as we have over the two and a half centuries since Wesley's day. In fact, conflicts have plagued Methodism in nearly every quadrennium (the four-year period from one General Conference to another).

In 1844, the Methodists assembled in General Conference couldn't agree on the interpretation of scripture regarding slavery. Many delegates, particularly from the South, believed scripture clearly supports the institution of slavery, while other delegates, mainly from the North, argued that scripture understood through Jesus Christ clearly calls for freedom. At that time, 16 years before the Civil War, the tension tore the church in half. Following the split, the Methodist Episcopal Church and the Methodist Episcopal Church South maintained separate denominations until they were able to reunite in 1939. Do you think that wasn't a wilderness wandering for the church? The pain of splitting caused great soul-searching as faithful Christians struggled for 95 years to follow God's will for Methodism. The wilderness wandering didn't stop then, either; the Central Conference was established to keep black-majority congregations and pastors from being part of the white-majority conferences.

In 1869, the first women applied for ordination in the Wesleyan denominations, but they were soundly rejected. The women trying to gain representation as lay members to General Conference fought for church recognition at the same time the women's suffrage movement was fighting for the right to vote. Here again a major part of the denomination was forced to its own wilderness wanderings. Lay women were finally given full laity rights in 1900. Women in the U.S. were allowed to vote in 1920. Women were ordained as full elders in 1956. These "wilderness wanderings" kept the church from reaching its full potential. When the church prevents some of its people from participating fully, it robs itself of these people's gifts.

If we remember the way the Exodus prepared the Israelites for the Promised Land, that may help us to see how today's wilderness wanderings are beneficial. As we face change and transition, we can learn from it. We must dig deep, to search ourselves to discover who we really are, and identify where God is in this.

Goodbye to Egypt

The Israelites longed for the leeks and melons of Egypt. In the rural areas where I was raised, although watermelons and cantaloupe are delicious, we longed for the ripe red tomatoes of summer. But for Moses' people, the longings were for more than refreshing foods in a land of thirst. Think about what those longings indicated: a willingness to give up freedom and return to slavery in order to eat well.

How quickly we forget the bad parts, if only we can return to the good. It's a variation on the Return to Eden that so many of our stories highlight. Was it really Eden? Or do we just remember it as Paradise?

We do that in our churches constantly. We wish for the "glory days," when nearly everyone we knew spent Sunday morning at church. We remember full worship services, and Sunday schools so crowded that sometimes we had to start additional classes. We remember when money was not so tight, and one church after another had new buildings or educational wings or other improvements. We remember when we could make fairly accurate assumptions about most of the people in our small towns being members of one church or another.

Immediately after World War II, people flocked to the churches, and it seemed we were sharing the gospel almost without effort. We began with gratitude for the end of war, and then so many Americans moved into college on the G.I. bill, moved to suburbia, built houses, and found decent jobs. We gave thanks again for the fulfillment of the American Dream. Why would it ever be different?

Through the '50s and '60s, as baby boomers filled schools and churches and their parents settled into comfortable lives—if not *Leave It to Beaver*, at least close enough—the churches seemed healthy, especially the mainline churches, the Protestant backbone of American Christianity. We thought we were getting close to God's will for us.

When the Israelites looked back to their glory days, they remembered the melons but conveniently forgot what it's like to make bricks when you have no straw. When we church members look back to our glory days of the '50s and '60s of the 20th Century, we tend to conveniently ignore the accompanying problems.

People of color didn't seem to exist for most of us, except perhaps as a far-off movement we might cheer on, without getting personally involved. Blacks in America lived under Jim Crow laws in the South and subtler kinds of racism in the North. Seldom did we see them in the mainly-white churches. Martin Luther King called 11:00 a.m. on Sunday morning "the most segregated hour in America." These were not "glory days" for people of color, nor for other groups that faced discrimination.

Back in America's Egypt of the 1960s:

- Disabled family members were often sent to institutions or kept hidden at home.
- Mental health problems, substance abuse, and domestic violence, were issues most people, including politicians, chose to ignore.

- Women who wanted a larger role in society were branded as "troublemakers" or "uppity women."
- Judaism, Islam, and other minority faith communities were given less credence and support for their worship practices than the Christian majority.
- Although LGBTQ persons existed in every neighborhood, there were very few tiny pockets where they could be open about their sexuality.

It's hard to move forward if we only want to live in the past. If we would avoid the yearning to live in the "glory days," we must begin by honestly realizing what they were like.

Refined by Fire

No one is eager to go through the fire, even if we know at the outset that fire is necessary. The Children of Israel had to wander for forty years, a time of purification, before they could be ready for the Promised Land. The Torah says the older generation was so sinful that the group could not be purified until all the oldsters had died off (Numbers 32:13). But if we understand the power of wilderness, we know that individuals and groups need the purification which results from it.

Jesus wasn't ready for his ministry until he spent time alone in the wilderness. We often use Lent as a time for Christians to discover the cleansing and transformation that can come after our own 40-day discipline. Conversely, uncertainty, grief, deprivation, and pain can lead to a loss of faith. Like the wandering Israelites, we can't focus on hope for a future. The marvel is how often these wanderings and personal Exodus stories become the source of spiritual strength and inner transformation. By struggling through, we transition into a deeper faith.

After a trial, people often say, "Oh, it was hard while I was going through it! But it brought me to a renewed faith, a new peace, a new spirit." Only at that point can we appreciate the benefits of the wilderness.

From the Wilderness to the Future

The denomination continues to struggle. Each of us wonders what the long-term effects of the 2019 General Conference will be. Even during the gathering, many feared the United Methodists Church would split into two denominations. Instead, the decision made there has led to a pregnant pause. While the future seems hazy, we wait to see what a transition will look like. This is certainly a wilderness wandering, so what is it preparing us to do and be?

Some of our folk will undoubtedly choose a different denomination. We wish them well and hope they will be blessed in carrying the gospel and sharing love on whatever path they take.

Some who have equally good reason to leave, are declaring not to give up on the United Methodist Church. But still they ask, "What can we do now?" Perhaps the real challenge is to seek to understand the teachings of the wilderness. What would Moses say to those of us who long to see our church fully transition, and perhaps transform into something new?

With that in mind, I ask:

1) *Can we become more understanding of the reasonable and faithful Methodists who have come to a different place on these issues?*

We have spent years arguing issues because of our various interpretations of scripture and diverse ways of seeking God's will through Christ. We have all known times in which we felt reconciled to God, but can we be reconciled to each other, even when we disagree with our brothers and sisters in the faith? We talk about loving each other, but this includes trying to understand those whose beliefs are different from our own. Can we discuss our differences without rancor?

2) *Can we transition into a church that is more sensitive to those who have been hurt?*

This is hard. None of us wants to think we are part of a group that would hurt others deliberately. Yet, we have LGBTQ persons both within and outside the church who have spoken strongly about how the church has hurt them. When they are excluded from full participation in the church; when others want to change them or speak of their sexuality as a sin; when they are discriminated against because they are wrongly thought to be pedophiles or spreading AIDS, they are hurt. In addition, family and friends of the LGBTQ persons may feel unable to share freely within the church, because they don't know what reaction they'll receive. Clearly, more education and discussion on these matters are needed.

In all this, we must not forget the more traditional members who feel that their church wants to discard or ignore certain deeply valued scriptures. Simply throwing arguments at them will not change minds. In fact, when people are hurt, they tend to cling to their ideals even more. Can we transition into a church that continues to be in conversation, that is willing to talk this out until we all understand each other?

3) *Can we continue to take the gospel to all the world?*

How will we continue to grow as a church in places with differing cultural understandings of homosexuality and marriage? How will we continue to minister to members of the LGBTQ community? How will we reach this country's young adults and unchurched if our teachings seem out of date?

The wilderness wanderings of the Children of Israel purified them so that they were ready to go into the Promised Land to create a holy nation. We are wandering, and we are troubled. Are we purified yet? Is there hope for us? What will it look like when we transition into the Promised Land?

About Loss

How do you deal with the one that got away?

One the most important lessons we can learn in life is how to deal with loss. If your heart was set on a particular side winning at the 2019 Special General Conference, you may be feeling a certain degree of loss right now. Even if you backed the Traditional Plan, you may be looking at half a fish and wondering when the UMC will be whole again, or wondering who to blame for the incomplete nature of the decision.

Real Christian spiritual development isn't about being graceful winners, but about remaining faithful and at peace in both the fruitful times and the times of loss.

SIX

Reality, Loss, and Spirituality

BY JOE FORT

O ur denomination continues to be in uncharted territory. To some persons, the decision of the Special General Conference to back the Traditional Plan implies a sense of finality to the denomination's debate about homosexuality. Congregations and individuals on both sides of the issue will choose to exit, and not all of them will leave quietly. Some will be upset, angry, and pointing accusing fingers on their way out. Even if the pastor, the most readily visible face of the UMC, has sought to lead the church with dignity and grace, he or she may incur a portion of this wrath. To say this possibility will not be fun is an understatement.

But beyond the potential loss of both members and attendees, as people leave, so also leave their offerings. Churches that have been accustomed to providing ministry and funding operating costs at a certain level will now be faced with lower giving that renders previous standards of service impossible. It will not be the long-predicted, so-called, "death tsunami" that has already appeared for many congregations in the UMC. This death tsunami has been, for most, actually a routine tide simply going out: aging constituents, accompanied by gradual declines in membership and worship attendance. The days ahead for us could be more like a real tsunami. It will be a tidal wave that threatens to wipe out large segments of a congregation all at once.

So how will we respond to these times as pastors and church leaders? As we reflect upon how to cope with loss, I would like to suggest that we begin by considering our inward responses to these losses. Only then I believe will we be in a position to talk about possible outward responses, that is, how we seek to lead in our churches when the foundations seem to be crumbling around us.

Our Inward Response

Even reasonably humble pastors and church leaders swallow hard at the prospect of apparent failure. We tend to take failure and loss personally. True, the Church is the Body of Christ. It is not supposed to be of this world. However, the Church has always been comprised of imperfect sinners, and those in leadership are no exception. It has always been easy to measure our self-worth by means of the relative success through various metrics. Congregations and church leaders alike do this. If the local church is growing in membership, attendance, and financial strength, we feel good about ourselves. If we complete a successful building program and have a nice new facility on our property, our self-esteem is likewise boosted.

In a given parish, steady growth or expansion may not be

easy to come by, however. Over the past generation, as we have moved more and more into a secular, unchurched culture, we have tended to lower our expectations. Simply maintaining becomes the new norm of success.; that is, if we can just keep holding our own, not seeing attendance or giving slip much, we are doing okay. In other words, we have a "moral victory' if we only tread water and hang in there.

Having become accustomed to such a world, it is easy to see how sudden, dramatic losses of people and finances can throw us into emotional turmoil. We may try hard to rationalize and intellectualize what is going on ("After all, this isn't our fault, is it?"), yet what we keep telling ourselves in our heads does little to change the punch we are feeling in our gut. It still hurts, and our pithy, "elevator speech" public comments don't change anything.

I enrolled in seminary at age twenty-two. I was in the first wave of ministry candidacy in the United Methodist Church. I had met a few times with my pastoral mentor, but when I went off to school, he was 300 miles away. In order to finish my exploring candidacy process, the seminary's bishop-in-residence was assigned to be my new mentor. His name was O. Eugene Slater.

During one of our conversations, I happened to ask Bishop Slater out of the blue, "What happens if you spend many years in ministry and come to realize that many of the dreams you had when you were younger are not going to come true?" Specifically, I think I had in mind the kinds of career ambitions that many young pastors tend to have. Bishop Slater paused for a moment and then responded, "You need a strong devotional life." That was all he said.

Those words were pretty much lost on me at the time, but as I have gotten older, I have come to realize how true they are. Nothing can keep us afloat during turbulent times like a resolute faith in Christ, constant abiding in the Word of God, and much prayer.

Over the past twenty years, or so, I have also come to value the power of the great spiritual classic writers to enrich my life and add to my understanding of the faith. I have read and re-read Thomas A'Kempis, Francois Fenelon, John Wesley, Andrew Murray, Dietrich Bonhoeffer, Thomas Merton, Henri Nouwen, and a number of others. Enduring insights such as theirs do far more to build me up than the latest "how to" books on ministry, many of which tend to be shallow and devoid of serious reflection. "You need a strong devotional life," the old bishop replied to my question. I say "amen" to that … now more than ever.

I would add that it is very critical right now for pastors in chaotic, stressful ministry situations to clearly understand that none of us can go it alone. We have all been reminded of this over and over, but are often guilty of trying to tough hard times out on our own with inadequate support systems in place. I am preaching to myself here. I am as bad as anyone about trying to gut out adversity until I become completely drained. Years ago, a church administrative assistant gave me a sign to hang in my office. Her nickname for me was "the Big Kahuna." (I am thankful it was not much worse!). The sign said this: "Big Kahuna parking only … all others will be wiped out!" I still like to fancy myself as being the Big Kahuna, but too often find that I am the one wiping myself out!

Times aren't getting easier for those of us who are called to be spiritual leaders over a flock. The days and months ahead could be very rocky indeed. We need to seek out trustworthy confidants with whom we can discuss what we are going through. These should be persons who not only care for us but are also willing to speak the truth in love to us when necessary.

Practicing appropriate self-care is not about putting our needs first. Rather, it is about understanding that we are of little value to the Kingdom of God when we permit ourselves to become beat-up, worn-out, empty shells. We must be good stewards to our emotional, physical, and spiritual selves so that we will be most fit for service to God. This is not about self-centeredness. This era in our Church, and the demands it will place upon us as leaders, requires us to be deliberate and intentional about practicing self-care.

Our Outward Response

Striving to maintain a calm, non-anxious presence is easier said than done- especially when it feels as if we are sailing in the middle of a storm, the ship's mast has broken off, and the wheel isn't steering the rudder anymore. The handful of ideas I am about to suggest are not earth-shaking; you've no doubt heard them before, but we need to keep reminding ourselves of them. They should be notes posted on our personal refrigerators for constant reference as we move into the future.

First, there are likely to be worried and upset people around you. Not all the angry people will leave the church. Some of them will remain, without keeping a lid on their emotions or filtering their speech. When people are beset by fear and anxiety, they are not going to be at their best. While this is unpleasant for a pastor or leader, remember that you did not instigate these situations. Your outward reaction, however, has a lot of power to help or hurt.

Many of the great spiritual writers throughout history have talked about the concept of "detachment." It may be tempting to think that detachment means becoming aloof and unfeeling, but this is not true. It means keeping a distance from unhelpful responses to the world around us. It means having the humility to refrain from judging people or taking things personally. It means not leading with our egos out front. Praying for detachment from our pride, oversensitivity, and snap judgments, is a major project for most of us! But in these times, it is also a very important spiritual goal for all of us to seek.

Just as it is vital that we strive to remain loving, mature, and Christ-like as pastors, I believe it is also essential that in this time we lean upon our key leaders in the church who have the same qualities. Pastors need to learn early on that every good layperson is not gifted to take on just any potential leadership position in the church. Not everyone who would make a good Trustee will also make a good Pastor-Parish Relations Committee member. Not every person on the Missions Committee would be well equipped to serve on the Finance Committee. This is just common sense, but it is sometimes easy to forget when the time for nominations rolls around!

During stormy times, those who are the most mature, wise, and Christ-like among our lay members should be the ones we seek out to help steer the church's ship. Folks whose feathers are easily ruffled or are quick to react out of fear and anxiety may have many enduring qualities otherwise, but could make things worse for their church if asked to lead in roles where those traits might frequently surface.

At this point, I would like to suggest another idea which I hope you will take seriously. For several years, you may have been serving a congregation which has been relatively healthy and stable. Although your appointment itself is the same, the nature of the appointment is now rapidly changing. Even though you are the same pastor with the same congregation, you must now understand that much of the work that lies before you in the near term must be more akin to "intentional interim" work.

Over the past decade, some conferences have taken positive steps to train and utilize interim pastors in ministry settings that have been traumatized or otherwise disrupted. In the past, new pastors were often just appointed to these places and left to fend for themselves. At best, it was very hard for them, and at worst, the results became disastrous. Thankfully, a number of our denominational leaders and conferences have come to understand that intentional interim ministry can be a valuable asset if used strategically.

What we need to grasp is that this sort of ministry may be the norm for the majority of pastoral settings over the months ahead. Furthermore, we are the ones who must do this ministry. There may be no backup plan. If we were to move to another appointment right now, we would only be inheriting another such interim ministry with its own bundle of needs.

Pastors and annual conferences must fully appreciate this reality and do the best they can to prepare for it. Training and coaching will need to be provided and sought out. Most of us do not have enough tools for doing interim ministry in a parish where the foundations have been shaken. It will be wise for us to admit this and seek out help where needed.

Major losses in giving and personnel must force us to accept that the church we are pastoring now is not what it used to be, perhaps not even in the recent past. This will be hard to deal with, especially for congregations who tend to dwell in the "good old days," instead of living in the present moment! Pastors and other key leaders must accept the new reality before meaningful decisions can be made about the present and future course of ministry in our churches.[1]

The loss of worship attendees will force practical decisions to be made. For example, no matter what the seating capacity of a given worship space – be it 80 or 800 – there is a relative "floor" worship attendance below which engaged, participatory worship begins to feel less inviting and warm. The larger the worship space, the more critical this issue becomes. Thus, some congregations may need to consider combining worship services to maintain a positive worship environment. None of us likes the prospect of cutting back in ministry, but a congregation that experiences a significant decline in worship attendance may need to actively embrace this idea.

Other programmatic decisions may have to be made, depending upon the present resources as opposed to the former resources. Such decisions can impact the church's Sunday School, youth and children's ministries, Vacation Bible School, and other areas of ministry. It is one thing to have less money on hand to fund such ministries. It is another thing to recognize that the congregation's volunteer resources may have also been seriously eroded. The prospect of losing willing helpers for programs will be a part of our new reality.

In the United States, thousands of United Methodist congregations see fewer than twenty persons in worship on a given

Sunday. For these churches, the loss of just one or two extended families could mean the end. They will either have to close their doors after many decades of service in a community, or possibly merge with a neighboring congregation.

Other thousands of churches have managed barely to stay afloat as full-time pastoral charges, either by themselves or on a multi-point charge. Many of these congregations, due to fewer folks and less giving, will be forced to become part-time appointments. These downward trends have been with us for a long time, but up to now, they have been gradual, with the tide going out slowly. Now we could be facing a storm surge.

Of course, reduced funding resources will necessitate churches of all sizes to make difficult decisions. Many small congregations learned to function in financial survival mode a long time ago, with barely enough money to keep the doors open and pay a small salary to the pastor. Like those churches that lose active participant households, the loss of one or two generous contributors may spell the end. Again, we have been dealing with slow bleeding on this front for many years. Now, however, the bleeding could become much more profuse.

As leaders, we must meet the problem of seriously impaired financial resources head-on and proactively. Unless our parish already survives month to month, it would be best not to wait until there is literally no money left to pay the current bills before we address the challenges before us. Significantly reduced giving will force hard choices.

Larger membership congregations often have roughly half of their total operating budgets tied up in personnel costs. There will be no way to make major reductions in overall church expenses unless the staff is included. It is one thing to trim down program budgets; it is more difficult to let staff go. Especially when people are involved, the best path is always compassion and fairness. There are no easy solutions here, only choices between more and somewhat less pain. Trying to keep support systems in place for all of those affected by these decisions – both those whose positions are being downsized or eliminated, and those who must make these tough calls – will be important.

The financial rubber may finally hit the road when the congregation can no longer afford to pay the pastor's salary at the same level as before. If this happens, we must respond with soul-searching and prayer. Hopefully, your district superintendent will be able to offer meaningful and unbiased advice.

The D.S should also be available to meet with church leaders to graciously discuss constructive options for the future of the charge.

Pastoral Change

As pastor, if financial realities cause you to move to another charge, ideally you will have established a helpful interim-type ministry so that the congregation can continue to operate smoothly. Bear in mind, however, that your leaving will constitute another serious loss for the church, especially if you have enjoyed a faithful, fruitful pastorate there, All deserve to be actively supported throughout this process.

Do not forget that just as we have only one chance to make a good first impression, there is also only one chance to make a good last impression. A pastor may be hurt on the inside, but not leaving well can only further tear up a church body that is already reeling. Please do not permit your final days with your flock to leave a bad taste in their mouth, or to become a source of regret in your own life down the line.

We should never forget the importance of forgiveness. Today there are many angry, upset, and anxious pastors, leaders, and members in our churches. We are not always kind and patient with one another. Hurtful words are being spoken. We all bear the mutual wounds of our un-Christlike words and deeds.

I imagine that each of you even now has a long list you need to pray over. You must forgive individuals who have treated you inconsiderately, and all parties – including those within the UMC – that you feel are causing you and your church unnecessary pain. You must furthermore seek forgiveness from those whom you have hurt, whether unwittingly or not. Without forgiveness, there will be no healing for you, your congregation, or for our denomination as we move into the future.

The United Methodist Church, which blossomed in the years after World War II into a large, mainline denomination, has been declining numerically for several decades. What will become of us over the months and years ahead, only God knows. But we must remember that the Church has always been subject to change. Just compare our present church with the early decades of the Wesleys.

God has a plan for the UMC, but a generation from now, it may look very different from what it was back in the 1950's, or even the 1990's! Still, there will a future – and it will be a good one – if we can be faithful to our calling of making disciples for Jesus Christ in the midst of a lost and hurting world. All that is now going on around us should compel us to rededicate ourselves to that calling ... this is our Great Commission.

In a room where
people unanimously maintain
a conspiracy of silence,
one word of truth
sounds like a pistol shot.

— Czesław Miłosz
Polish-American poet, social commentator, and diplomat.

SEVEN

What Would Paul Say?

BY BILL KEMP

The story goes that an old-school evangelist was preaching away one hot summer evening. The small backwoods church was only half-full and the response to the message was less than enthusiastic. Nevertheless, the evangelist preached on. He launched into a list of sins and temptations to be avoided. He preached about adultery, and then asked if he could have an *amen*. There was silence, except for an elderly woman in the back pew, far end, close to the window. She said, "Preach it, brother!" So, he went on. He preached about gambling and got another amen from her. He preached about the dangers of drink, and she hollered, "Amen!"

Then he made mention of how he himself had been saved from the evils of chewing tobacco. The old woman was silent. She spit out the window and whispered to the person beside her, "Now he's just meddling."

I tell that old story because it says something about evangelists. The Apostle Paul was an old-school evangelist. He went from place to place preaching the good news about Jesus Christ. In fact, when I was in seminary, I learned about a sermon format called "the Roman Road." It is a thematic arraignment of the key points of Paul's Letter to the Romans. It begins with the understanding that we all have sinned and fallen short of what God has intended for us. It proceeds to tell how we can be made right again through faith. The reason this evangelistic structure is so effective is because many people intuitively sense a need to be doubly saved: both from a former life of sin, and to a new "saved" life with the hope of God's glory.

The conversion of a violent gang member into a peaceful, "born again" Christian is the kind of story that supports evangelistic fervor. The Apostle Paul repeatedly used his own conversion story to great effect. He says, "I persecuted the church of God. But by the grace of God I am what I am…" (I Corinthians 15:9-10). As a strict Pharisee before his conversion, Paul didn't have any of the old lifestyle sins that evangelists often list today. He didn't drink or cuss or chew or hang around with those that do. He couldn't tell a hair-raising tale of sexual immorality. There was, though, one sin in his past that made Paul fit for hell before Jesus saved him. He hated people who believed differently than he did. In fact, he thought that those who followed Christ should be hunted down, imprisoned, and put to death. Coming to faith, for the Apostle Paul, was not a simple matter of replacing his old hatred of Christians with a new hatred of those who weren't Christian. Instead, he came to see love as the driving force behind real Christian conversion.

So, what would the Apostle Paul say about LGBTQ people? His letters, which make up half of the New Testament, are predominantly concerned with evangelism. Even when he deals with practical church matters, such as whether women should be allowed to speak in worship, he frames his advice in terms of evangelism. He doesn't ask what is theologically pure; instead, he asks, "What will allow more people to hear about the grace of God?" Paul abandons the legalistic tone of his Pharisaic training and says, "To those not having the law I became like one not having the law... so as to win those not having the law" (I Corinthians 6:22). Looking through the whole of Paul's letters, as well as Luke's remembrances of him in Acts, a picture emerges of an evangelist constantly reshaping his list of sins to fit his audience's perceptions. If Paul were alive today, doing altar calls in San Francisco, I doubt he would call to the stage a former homosexual who had successfully completed a conversion therapy program. In fact, a modern Paul might see a similarity between the gay-to-straight conversion therapy programs that some Christians call for, and the emphasis on adult men being circumcised that some of his contemporaries were advocating (Galatians 5:2-6).

This is not to say that Paul was ambivalent about morality or changed his definition of sin depending upon the situation. Rather, Paul's pragmatic concern for reaching his audience always outweighed his internal beliefs about right and wrong. Further, for reasons that will be discussed later, Paul didn't think the church had both the time to convince people that the behavior they thought was natural was wrong, and the time to convince people that God had acted to save them. Famously, he said that his only mission was to preach Christ crucified.

I don't know how comfortable you were with the example I used at the beginning of this chapter. Part of what identifies the United Methodist church with the mainstream of American religion is our acceptance of the fact that faith in God does not come to every individual in the same way. The dramatic "I used to be this kind of sinner, and now I am that kind of saint, by the grace of God" evangelistic story only resonates with a small portion of our members. Most members identify with the gradual unfolding of God's grace in their lives. They can't speak of a sinful past that they abandoned on the day they met Jesus. The thing that unites us, however, is a profound gratitude for the undeserved grace of God in our lives. Paul understood this.

Do we as United Methodists, like the tobacco-chewing woman above, simply disregard our evangelist Paul when he says something that we find inconvenient? No. I believe our intent is very different. We desperately need to recover Paul's evangelistic drive and passion. We can't, however, simply carbon-copy Paul of Tarsus for the digital age. When we disregard I Corinthians 14:34-35 and invite women into worship leadership, we aren't discounting Paul as a mere meddler. We are honoring his unique ear for what the particular church at Corinth needed. We are saying that Paul's love for Christ and the church still inspires us. But discovering what Paul would say today requires more than just reading his letters literally.

* Reflect or discuss: *Many people today consider the Apostle Paul to be sexist. Does thinking of him as a pragmatist, someone who is guided by practical considerations, allow us to see his words in a different light?*

Obviously, It's a Sin

The Apostle Paul's form of evangelism, as we have noted, is dependent upon placing before his readers a list of sins that they can instinctively and intuitively recognize as wrong. This is what he did in Romans 1:18-32, a passage that begins with the ominous words, "The wrath of God is being revealed against all godlessness and wickedness..." He constructed his list very carefully. The Roman church included both Jews and gentiles. Paul wanted to talk about sins that both cultural groups would find obvious. He couldn't, for instance, say that eating pork was a sin, even though he had learned as a child that it was important to obey Moses and eat only kosher food. Nor does he criticize the Roman Gentiles for going to the theater or watching gladiators fight. *Game of Thrones* fans can be relieved that Paul didn't forbid the watching of shows with gratuitous sex and violence. Instead, Paul constructed his list around two areas of sin that human beings universally feel shame about: idolatry (making something trivial into your god) and sexual immorality (making an act of love trivial). Paul notes how the two are similar and relates both to our broken relationship with God. [1]

If the Apostle Paul were alive today and writing this letter to our capital, he might well speak about idolatry and sexual immorality. He would cite different examples, though. In the Roman Empire, gods fashioned after animals filled the temples, and good citizens were expected to worship the statue of the current emperor with a pinch of incense (Romans 1:23). Today, we don't worship our president, nor do we go to the zoo to practice our religion. Paul is banking on the fact that the thoughtful people of his day felt a certain shame about worshiping the emperor Nero, or the python at Delphi. It is obvious that the created world belongs to a much higher power. We ought to feel a similar shame today when we express an idolatrous worship of food and alcohol or athletes and celebrities.

Similarly, in Paul's day, homosexual practice often involved the rape of slaves. Wealthy men were allowed to be pedophiles, and prostitution was considered a normal part of pagan society. For Paul, accepting Christ meant being converted away from these shameful acts. The first chapter of Romans is an eloquent reflection on how sexual violence and the trivializing of our interpersonal relationships has forced the loving God to abandon us to the soul vacancy that comes with one-night stands. Paul's basic argument has only become stronger over time. Twenty centuries of human progress, and our news is still filled with shameful stories of rape, human trafficking, and the sexual misconduct of our political and religious leaders.

Note these three things:

First, United Methodists agree that sexual immorality is sinful and a profound indicator of how fallen our world is. It is common, however, for those who are younger and more progressive not to speak of a specific act as sinful when there isn't a victim. Some United Methodists feel that whatever two consenting adults do within the privacy of their home is not a religious matter. Adultery is wrong, both because it violates the Ten Commandments and because it is rarely, if ever, without a victim. United Methodist leaders are held to the standard of "celibacy in singleness." Oddly, we don't require this of our widowed seniors who are seeking to retain Social Security benefits. We rightly tell our youth groups that premarital sex is wrong because it is rarely a healthy or safe way to explore our sexuality. Few of us, however, would class it as a sin like adultery. Many clergy-persons chafe at the fact that our Discipline places a higher standard on their sexual practices than on the laity. Clergy need to be held accountable for misconduct. They don't need to be housed in goldfish bowls. Further, in states where both same-sex marriage and divorce are legal, why do we expect our Conference Board of Ordained Ministry to consider one to be morally disqualifying for ministry and not the other?

I've gone a bit into the weeds in the above paragraph because I want you to note that sexual ethics is a matter of degrees. It is unfair to assume that someone who supports LGTBQ rights is also less serious about living a biblical lifestyle. Since the Apostle Paul's time, nothing has changed in the church's disgust for those who are sexually immoral, pedophiles, or who practice polyamory. Where immorality rears its ugly head, however, changes from time to time. If we want to learn from Paul, then we must adopt a more pragmatic approach to human sexuality.

Second, in the three places that Paul directly speaks about homosexuality (Romans 1:26-27, I Corinthians 6:9-10, and 1 Timothy 1:9-10), he is speaking as an evangelist, making a list. Many United Methodists today, like the elderly woman above, sit in the back of the church and nod our heads as we hear the Apostle Paul speak about idolatry, greed, gossiping, murder, the lack of respect for authority, etc. Then Paul says that women shouldn't speak in church, or that slave-holding is a matter of individual conscience (Philemon 8-16), or that homosexuality is a sign of humanity's depraved nature and we say, "Now he's meddling." Making a list to express how one's lifestyle changes after salvation is a tricky business. Each generation has to develop its own understanding as to where the boundaries around sin lie. God gave to Moses ten words — a decalogue —

as ethical commandments. By being succinct, God left for coming generations the work of determining what exactly is forbidden by "thou shall not commit adultery," "no murder," and "don't covet."

Third, the Apostle Paul, like many evangelists today, says it's common sense that these activities are wrong (Romans 1:19). Paul was a natural theologian. Like C.S. Lewis in *Mere Christianity*, Paul argues that our individual conscience is both God-given and universal, that is, understood in exactly the same way by all cultures. No one needs to be taught that stealing is wrong. Keeping the sabbath and adultery, however, seem to be less universally understood. Natural Theology sometimes breaks down when one crosses from one culture into another. If people of integrity and good character may feel no inner conflict regarding actions that others, of another culture, feel is wrong, then obviously natural theology doesn't apply to the matter under discussion. I might be appalled by the idea of eating raw fish, and yet I know many people with high moral standards who love sushi. We must be careful and open-minded when applying our gut-level instincts to both matters of taste and human sexuality. Many LGBTQ people say that their conscience pains them when they contemplate their own participation in a heterosexual relationship, or when they assume a gender identity that doesn't feel natural to them.

* Reflect or discuss: *How persuaded are you by the Christian leaders of our time who say that homosexuality is "unnatural"? What type of evidence would be persuasive?*

The Law of Love

As mentioned before, Paul is the kind of evangelist who speaks about two changes happening to us when we receive the grace of God through Jesus Christ: a change is lifestyle and change in our ability to love. In another of his letters, Paul is concerned about the reputation of the church in Corinth. He has received word that some church members are taking other members to court. He has also heard rumors of sexual immorality among people who profess themselves to be Christians. He says, "Or do you not know that wrongdoers will not inherit the kingdom of God? Do not be deceived: Neither the sexually immoral nor idolaters nor adulterers nor men who have sex with men nor thieves nor the greedy nor drunkards nor slanderers nor swindlers will inherit the kingdom of God" (I Corinthians 6:9-10).

Obviously, Paul is concerned about the church's witness. If nonbelievers see church members being vicious towards each other in court and committing immoral acts, then why would anyone believe their message about Christ? The list of embarrassments he provides could well have been written to any of a number of United Methodist congregations today. We do not diminish Paul's words by taking out of this list the final reference to homosexuality. The nonbelievers around us no longer consider it an immoral act. Instead, the weight of Paul's criticism of this particular congregation involves their failure to be led by the Holy Spirit into a more loving lifestyle. This desire to see them change their ways leads later in the book to his famous chapter on Love, I Corinthians 13.

Even though there is no evidence of Paul ever hearing these

words, he would agree fully with Jesus' final command to his disciples:

> *By this everyone will know that you are my*
> *disciples, if you love one another…*
> *My command is this: Love each other as I have*
> *loved you. Greater love has no one than this:*
> *to lay down one's life for one's friends.*

- John 13:35 & 15:12-13

Paul saw a direct connection between the love that Jesus showed us with his death on the cross, and the love Christians ought to show for each other. His letters display his concern for unity in the church. Here again, if the Apostle Paul were to wade into our current debate about the LGBTQ issue, he would be concerned about both our unity and our witness. He would chide us for failing to treat each other with respect. He might even have a word to say about the United Methodist Church's current lack of interest in ecumenical unity. Paul would not be pleased to see local churches competing with each other, or denominations failing to extend bonds of friendship and fellowship to each other. In light of this, he might find any schism within the United Methodist church to be small potatoes compared to the full disunity of the body of Christ. It's a matter of having a global perspective, something Paul had long before it was trendy.

* Reflect or discuss: *What would Paul say to your local church?*

Context

Perhaps more than with any other biblical author, it is a dangerous thing to take the Apostle Paul out of context. And yet, it's so tempting. Later in I Corinthians, Paul writes, "It is good for a man not to have sexual relations with a woman." This can be easily misconstrued. We need first to see these words in the context of the surrounding paragraph. Obviously, Paul is not saying that same-sex relationships are to be preferred. Instead, he is saying that marriage distracts the Christian disciple from serving the Lord full-time. For the record, I do *not* agree with Paul. To appreciate this paragraph, you need to read it in the context of Paul's other letters and his whole approach to Christian ministry.

Serious scholars will go a step further and note that some of the words Paul uses for sexual immorality can be translated in various ways. Not all of the passages where Paul seems to be condemning same-sex relationships correspond to the monogamous LBGTQ relationships we are discussing here. Further, biblical scholars debate which New Testament books are written by Paul, and which reflect the work of a later writer.

Further, by context, we also need to consider Paul's place in history. The church he was writing to was very different from our church today. The most remarkable thing about reading Paul in context is the way he expected Jesus to return again any day.[2] For Paul, the final page of human history was about to be turned, and passionately-discussed issues would soon become trivial. The only thing that mattered was preaching the good news of Jesus Christ. This is why Paul tells the Corinthians that they should marry only if they had to. In his words, "…it is better to marry than to burn with passion"(7:9b).

For Paul, then, having a long-term monogamous heterosexual relationship was a sign of weakness. Go back and read the entire seventh chapter of I Corinthians if you think I'm overstating this. Further, it might be interesting to see what Paul says about the word "weakness."

* Reflect or discuss: *There are those who speak of same-sex orientation as a weakness that a strong Christian can choose to ignore. What do you think?*

Paul says it Passionately

Finally, there are two things the Apostle Paul is passionate about: the saving death of Jesus Christ upon the cross, and his conviction that Christ would return again soon, bringing with him the resurrection of the dead and a new kingdom of peace and love. Some people believe that the United Methodist Church is in decline because it has abandoned the Holiness movement and is no longer a "conservative" church. I don't think that is the case. I think we have abandoned the spiritual passion that Paul evidenced. We no longer see the cross of Christ and the mystery of his passion to be central to our church life. Lent means little to us. Further, we no longer trust God to be in charge of human history. Admittedly, Paul was wrong to expect Jesus' second coming in the first century. He was right, though, to see Jesus Christ as the Lord of all things and the redeemer of all human beings (Philippians 2:5-11).

The Sunday after the conclusion of the 2019 Special General Conference, I visited a progressive congregation whose Facebook page stated how they would continue to be accepting LGBTQ people, no matter where the rest of the church was headed. They served communion and had an extended prayer time. A woman stood up and gave thanks for how the prayers of the people had carried her through a recent surgery. Other people stood to give witness to the effectiveness of prayer and the presence of the Holy Spirit in their daily lives. The music throughout the service touched my heart. Scripture was shared with an emphasis on how the ancient words were still relevant. In the preacher's message, he spoke honestly about his own personal grief. He went from that, however, to an effective interpretation of the day's scripture text, which I found both informative and inspired.

If I had traveled ten miles to the east that morning, I suspect I could have had an equally uplifting experience at a congregation led by conservatively minded clergy who have stated their support for the Traditional Plan. Both churches are growing and healthy. I point this out because it is often assumed that conservative churches are more likely to share the Apostle Paul's spiritual passion. While it is true that conservative churches are more likely to preach about Jesus' second coming, and speak more literally about his suffering, I have found people who are passionate about the grace of God in both traditional and contemporary worship settings. I believe the Apostle Paul is equally understood and respected by conservatives and progressives. Much of our debate about the affect of postmodern liberalism on the Christian zeal may be misguided.

Congregations that are spiritually passionate are more likely to thrive and make disciples for the transformation of their communities. The way to become more spiritually passionate as a church is to:

- Pray together as if prayer really mattered
- Read scripture as if it is relevant to daily life
- Witness about your faith with joy
- And do all that you can to make worship inspiring

(from "Ezekiel's Bones" by Bill Kemp)

The Apostle Paul emphasized these four things, not because he was theologically conservative, but because they were a natural part of his spiritually passionate lifestyle. They were his priorities and I think that the United Methodist Church would become more vital if we pursued these things rather than arguing about LBGTQ matters.

I have little doubt about what Paul would say if he were at the General Conference in Saint Louis. He would say, "The church doesn't have time for this." Paul expected Jesus' imminent return. He spoke of his own ministry as an athletic contest, as a race he intended to run. Sprinters don't have time for the long arc of history to bend towards justice (to quote Dr. Martin Luther King) Paul didn't know Jesus' return lay at least twenty centuries in the future. If he had, he might have shared our interest in working to end racism, classism, sexism, homophobia, etc. I often remind myself that the way I work out my salvation is more of a marathon. We, more than the Apostle Paul, are committed to the slow and intentional work of making disciples for the transformation of the world.

Let us not become weary in doing good, for
at the proper time we will reap a harvest
if we do not give up.

- Galatians 6:9

Human progress is neither automatic nor
inevitable... Every step toward the goal
of justice requires sacrifice, suffering,
and struggle; the tireless exertions and
passionate concern of dedicated
individuals.

— Dr. Martin Luther King

EIGHT

What's Love Got to Do with It?

BY KATHY MOORE

The root of our difficulty in discussing the LGBTQ issues lies in love and the question of whom we can love. As Christians, we embrace the concept of God as love and hope that our human love will reflect this. So often in our society, though, love is equated with sex or lust. People on a 13-week reality show on T.V. expect to find true love within a pool of 20 potential lovers. The movies show people on dates with full expectations of sleeping together before the night is over. Others assume that their marriage vow was, "As long as we both shall love," rather than "As long as we both shall live." How can we address the thorny question of "whom we are allowed to love" when we can't even make a more basic distinction between love, sexual practice, and lust?

We assume there is a universal norm. Good marriages begin with the mature choice of a suitable partner, are furthered by romantic love, and in time develop into a lifelong partnership, marked by authentic companionship and fidelity. They present a unified front to the world as a loving couple.

Sometimes, although everything in that last paragraph is present, the couple doesn't fit our preconceived norm. What if the two partners are of the same sex? Then what they have is often seen as lust. Many people still imagine that homosexuality is basically about pornography or promiscuity. Without any evidence, some people assume that pedophilia is more common among homosexuals.

So how do we talk about love? Christ's key revelation of God as love shows us that we must learn what God-ordained love is. We know Christians are called to love one another, and to love our neighbor, and even to love our enemy. What does Christ teach us about love that can help us in this current difficult discussion?

Can We Talk?

As hard as it is for us to have this conversation, the time has arrived for it. We don't like to talk about private matters, what goes on in someone's bedroom. We aren't voyeurs, after all. Yet our church has been struggling for nearly 50 years. [1]Every four years, we return to the fight at General Conference again, and every quadrennium we change some words or some policy, as we continue to debate the question of where the church should be regarding same-sex marriage and other related issues.

When I led a discussion at my church, I knew we had a wide diversity of opinions within our congregation. Several members had confided to me that a family member was gay or lesbian, and they were debating whether to continue in the church.

Other members clearly thought the Traditional Plan, with its rejection of homosexuality, was the right approach. Still others thought we had already spent too much time on these issues. Perhaps the majority, those who did not voice an opinion, would have said that the LGBTQ debate doesn't affect them very much.

As we went around a circle of nearly 50 members, sharing our own experiences, I was interested to hear one of our more conservative members say, "Well, I'd have to say I'm evolving on this issue. I'm not nearly at the same place I was 20 or 30 years ago." Following that, the majority of people around the circle had similar thoughts. Even some of the very conservative ones had changed had changed in their understanding. However, until I asked for a discussion group, most of them would have said it wasn't necessary. In fact, some of them challenged me beforehand, because I was "opening a can of worms." For many, this issue wasn't on the radar screen.

So, calling a special session of General Conference may be an important step in helping us discuss a tough issue. Now it's out in the open, forcing us to talk directly to each other.

In the midst of strong opinions and challenges to biblical interpretation, is it possible to actually discuss? How do we offer love and respect to another when we strongly disagree? Is it acceptable to agree to disagree, or are we so invested in our own argument that we can't stop until the other agrees with us?

Discussion doesn't have to come to agreement. We don't have to prove our point in order to win. I would suggest that a full discussion, kept to a tame voice rather than yelling, offered in respect rather than anger, would be a winning discussion. If both sides (or all sides) can end the discussion with a clear understanding of where the other is coming from, how the other arrived at these opinions, and respect rather than dislike for each other, we all win.

Who Can We Love?

If we can learn to talk in a caring way, can we also learn better how to love? Can we identify when love is "of God" and holy? Let's begin by acknowledging that we are not using words in the same way.

I have heard so many good Christians talk about homosexuality by saying, "Love the sinner, hate the sin." The people who believe so devotedly that they are following God's rule in this little saying do not at all realize how LGBTQ people hear that saying. LGBTQ people hear judgment. With every expression of their sexual self, even the simple act of attraction to another person, they are being told they are sinful. Other folks would say that LGBTQ persons are born that way, that sexual orientation is God-given, that living out our sexuality is not a sin.

On the other hand, for traditionalists, the issue concerns being the best person we can be. All of us have tendencies to sin that we must choose to override. They feel if it is true that God made people homosexual, then they are called to resist that urge.

The problem with the saying, "Hate the sin but love the sinner," is that we can't talk with each other when we aren't even using the same language. One side uses "sin" and "sinner," while the other says, "That's not a sin." The first group bristles, because they hear that as a statement that the homosexual is not a sinner, while the second group maintains that all are sinners, although living out one's God-given sexuality in a loving, caring way is acceptable.

How do we talk to each other if we can't agree on the language? How do we love each other if we're talking at cross purposes? Yes, we can love in a generalized, shallow way, but the love for Christian brothers and sisters needs understanding and trust to be deep. How does respect for other opinions grow?

What Does the Bible Say?

Probably the deepest divide between us has to do with the Bible. We argue over and over about the few verses in the Bible that apparently address homosexuality. We argue about what our 21st Century response should be. For some Christians, it matters very little what the Bible says about this issue. Through their own reasoning and experience, they conclude that the Bible authors didn't know about the kind of loving, caring, monogamous same-sex relationship that we often encounter in the LGBTQ community. The traditionalists believe this is dismissing God's word, while progressives contend that, while they honor and treasure the Bible, they don't regard every word as equally valid. For example, we don't regard the Bible as the last word on slavery, divorce, the role of women in the church, or dietary rules.

So, if we love and revere the Bible, how do we live in the 21st Century? We recognize that the ancient image of the earth and the wider universe no longer works for people who have flown in space and sent missions to the planets and stars. But what parts of the Bible do we still embrace, and what parts do we consider to be obsolete?

Can we love each other as people of the Book and followers of Christ? Can we accept the fact that we will not all agree on the details? Can love help us to recognize that the church's understanding of Scripture has changed through time? Can love help us be okay with that?

Marriage through the Ages

At the turn of the century, we would not have guessed that within a few short years, same-sex marriages would be legal all over the U.S. and in many other countries. This has created great alarm and anxiety throughout our churches. How is the church to treat the God-given gift of marriage? Can just anyone get married now? Are there no limits?

It is helpful to consider the history of marriage through the ages. It has not always been the same. In the days of the patriarchs, for example, the men were polygamous, having multiple wives as well as concubines and temple prostitutes. Abraham married Sarah,, whom he loved, but he lay with her slave-girl in order to have a son. As a very old man he married again. King Solomon had 700 wives and 300 concubines. Women had little voice, but the system was not questioned.

On through the centuries, most marriages were arranged, often because of dowry gifts or for political alliances. Sometimes young girls were married or betrothed at very young ages. Some marriages were made for economic reasons. Women needed the men for income, and the men needed housekeeping and child care.

Another reason for marriage was to provide for those without partners. Men whose wives died during childbirth often married soon after, needing someone to care for them and the children. Women who had lost their husbands and had no grown son could gain a home and food through a plural marriage. In fact, by Israeli law, the surviving brother was to marry the widow and give her children to carry on her late spouse's name and inheritance.

In the Book of Ruth, Boaz, an older man with no sons of his own, married Ruth, who bore the future grandfather of King David - the line that ultimately produced Jesus. The command to be fruitful and multiply (Genesis 1:28) underlies the Catholic prohibition of contraception. This continues to be observed in a world with over 7 billion souls living.

Marriage has changed in many respects since Bible times. Most people in the US today frown on plural marriages, concubinage and temple prostitution. We don't promise our little girls in marriage in order to gain money or political advantage. Women can choose to be single. We no longer think of procreation as the reason for marriage.

The Bible does, however contain stories about marriage for love. For example, Jacob served Laban for 14 years to marry Rachel, the woman he loved. He also married her sister Leah, and added sons through two slave-women. He clearly loved Rachel better than his other wives (Genesis 29).

Samuel's father also had a polygamous marriage. In this case Hannah was the beloved wife, even though she was barren and the culture then saw the failure to provide sons as grounds for a divorce (I Samuel 2). Similarly, in the New Testament, Zechariah and Elizabeth had a long loving relationship, even though their marriage didn't produce a child until their old age (Luke 1).

But marrying for love is a fairly new concept. Even though

Shakespeare gave us *Romeo and Juliet* in the 1500s, the idea of love as a prerequisite for marriage is only 150 to 200 years old. Today, anyone in the US can marry for love, even gays, as determined by the Supreme Court in 2015.

Christian Marriage

In modern times, we understand that marriage is the union of two people who want to share their whole lives together, because they love each other. Their bonding is to be a blessing—to each other, to their children, to family and friends, and ultimately to the wider world. We understand this to be God's desire for those who are not called to singleness. Christians who marry seek to live out this ideal.

Sexual intimacy is not simply for the sake of having children. At its best, it is a way God has created for human beings to join with each other for pleasure and closeness that cements the relationship. Intimacy helps a couple to be united, not just physically, but emotionally, mentally, and companionably. This seems to be God's intention; sadly, through the centuries up to today, we find countless cases of sex resulting from lust rather than love.

This ideal of marriage is theological, sealed through a religious ceremony with ritual words and actions. Marriage, however, is not always a religious act; for centuries, weddings were not celebrated in the church. The ritual words "To have and to hold…'til death do us part" were first used in the Church of England Prayer Book in 1662. People of faith consider marriage a gift of God, and the public declaration of the couple's commitment to each other expresses not only the joy and celebration of the community, but also the intention to have God as a part of the marriage.

Marriage rituals can be formal or informal, depending upon the culture, historical era, and place. At times, marriage plans were to be publicly proclaimed before the ritual so that other interested parties might have a chance to object. At other times, a marriage could be done privately by a couple speaking the necessary words. Slave communities celebrated when a couple "jumped the broom," literally jumping over a broom on the ground. Even though Christians consider marriage to be a sacred act, the rituals and customs contain numerous secular elements.

What makes us want a religious presence at a wedding? I have had couples who had no connection to any church but still wanted a church wedding. On some level, they seem to believe that God should be involved in our most important relationships.

If marriage is only secular, perhaps the rituals are insignificant. But if it is ordained by God to bring two people together in blessing to grow in love throughout their lives, then it is definitely a religious matter.

Is marriage, then, religious or secular? Truthfully, both. It is a legal event, sanctioned by the state, with wide ramifications for the couple. Some couples have no interest in the religious aspect, but still value marriage as a civil union. Those who are religious want God to bless their marriage, and to be a source of strength and guidance when troubles come.

The following elements are needed for a healthy marriage:

- Trust – on both sides
- Respect – to honor the other's personhood
- Equality – to build a true partnership
- Boundaries – within the union, each person is still a separate individual
- Empathy – to feel for the other, to be compassionate
- Intimacy – many kinds-sexual, physical, sensual, emotional, mental, companionable

* Now reflect on, or if you are in a small group, discuss: How could this list be made more complete?

Is there any item above that cannot exist in a same-sex union?

An Example

My friends Bill and Steve are a gay couple. They are faithful Christians and active in their church. Many years ago, Bill spoke to me about why he wanted a public marriage; -one that had God at its center. He concluded by saying:

When we first started speaking for our rights, people said, 'Oh, you're just all promiscuous and sinful.' So, we intentionally became more visible. We began to say, 'See, many of us are in monogamous relationships. We'd like to be married,' and they would say, 'Oh, no, not that. Gay marriage is going too far.' Steve and I have been together since the early '80s, and we'd love to be officially married to each other.

Now as I compare their relationship with the elements listed

above, I think Bill and Steve have one of the healthiest relationships around. Even though it doesn't conform to the definition
of marriage I grew up with, their love has many of the same
qualities I saw in my parents' 66-year marriage. So, it doesn't
seem odd to me that members of the LGBTQ community are
asking the United Methodist Church to bless their union.

NINE

What Then Should We Do?

BY BILL KEMP

O ne of my favorite TV shows is *Love It or List It* on HGTV. The show begins with a married couple complaining about their home. The house used to be cozy and cute, but now it just doesn't work for their family. Should they attempt to fix their house up or bite the bullet and move? Should they love it, after expensive and inconvenient repairs, or leave it for another house which may have its own problems? This is a lose - lose decision. If a simple and cheap renovation would have solved their problems, they would have done it long ago. Shopping for a new home may sound like fun, but it has its own set of complexities and hidden costs.

Enter the show's two hosts, a contractor and a realtor. Hillary, the renovation guru, promises to fix all the family's complaints by making changes to the current house. When she's done, Hillary promises, they'll *Love it*. David the realtor champions the opposite solution, leaving the mess and going somewhere new. He then shows the couple another house that meets all their expectations. Suddenly this couple has gone from facing a lose-lose situation to having a win-win opportunity. In each episode, Hillary and David do their magic so well that the couple goes from sadness to joy. They just have to decide between two good options: will they win by returning to their wonderfully reconfigured house, or by listing their home and moving to a new place?

Let's think of that show as an analogy for our current United Methodist Church. Like the couple in the show, our denominational house no longer works for us. The guest room, where we should be making new members feel comfortable, has thin walls. They can hear us arguing. The plumbing of our decision-making process leaks. The old foundation stones of our shared Wesleyan values no longer support the whole house. We can either undergo major renovations and reshape our current church to include both progressive and traditionally minded Methodists, or we can create a reasonable *List-It* process for those who must leave our denomination. The LBGTQ debate is not responsible for making our denominational home unlivable, but it is the one room that both sides hate. It is the place where our aging structure can no longer be patched together. It is where we are in danger of fatal collapse. The 2019 Special General Conference did not provide us with a way forward. It instead placed us in a *Love-It or List It* episode.

Okay, where are Hillary and David? We need magical TV personalities to flip our lose-lose dilemma into win-win. Unfortunately, we can't hire an outside consulting firm to rebrand us and put the "United" back together with Methodism. Neither can we, in this day and age, expect a single all-church gathering to provide a definitive answer that fits every ministry context and congregation. The 2019 Special General Conference did take the United Methodist Church out of the closet and put our debate on national television. There it lasted exactly one news cycle, or episode, on our culture's reality TV mindset. The world moves on; we methodically don't.

To take the analogy further, it's important to watch and learn from both Hillary the renovator, and David the realtor as they work the problem. A significant number of lifelong United Methodist members, clergy persons, and congregations, will choose to leave the denomination in the next few years. There may even emerge a plan for whole segments of the church to gracefully exit (let's hope it's better than Brexit). For those that stay, however, things will not be the same. All sides need to commit themselves to serious reformation. Staying in dysfunction is no longer an option.

In *Love it or List it*, the couple is faced with a lose-lose, "lesser of two evils" decision at the beginning of the show. It is unimaginable to them that either option will end well. Over the course of the episode, a transition occurs.

It has the following steps:

1) For the first time, the couple makes a comprehensive list of what is wrong with their current home. We should be thankful for the LGBTQ issue. It has allowed our generation to seriously face what is wrong with the United Methodist Church. Like all acts of confession and repentance, this reality check will ultimately prove to be of great worth.

2) As they look at new homes with David, the realtor, the couple is forced to face their fears about the future. For all of its faults, their old home provided a sense of security. Let's be honest: the United Methodist Church has become for most of us

a resting place. We retreat into our sanctuaries and find them, like the bar on *Cheers*, a place where *people are all the same, and everybody knows your name*. We seek refuge from our fears, rather than faith for the future God has for us.

3) As Hillary the renovator tears into the walls of the old homestead, she always finds some unexpected issue. "Did you know that none of your plumbing is up to code?" she asks. Unfortunately, we are not able to live in another church while our old denomination is being rebuilt. As the walls come down to fix the problem, we are forced into a time of wilderness. This time of *maximum mess* is very educational. The couple learns the difference between PVC and ABS pipe. In the wilderness of Exodus, God's people learned the Ten Commandments. What will we learn during our transition?

4) Before the couple can exit the no man's land of choosing between loving and listing it, they have to decide how to decide. In other HGTV shows, the host often plays the role of a counselor, helping the couple to see both sides of the issue and guiding their decision-making process. In *Love It or List It*, Hillary and David are too competitive to pretend to be transitional experts. Today, in the wilderness, we need to look for people willing to be neutral and act as wise guides. The great mantra for any successful transition is:

The process for making decisions is more important than any one decision.

5) In the end, whether they love the house that Hillary remade, or leave it for what David found far away, their choice will involve loss. Naming what we are losing is an important part of the process. Every significant transition is a grief process. The kids say goodbye to their friends at their old school. The

spare room where we used to keep our treasured keepsakes no longer exists in the renovated house. To have a significant and healthy church in the future, we must accept our losses and make peace with what we have to leave behind.

6) Our current episode will one day come to an end. The final step will be into a future that is unimaginable today. The magic of television is that the dysfunctional past and the marvelous future are only separated by 30 minutes. In real life, such transitions are measured in decades. Ten years from now, the United Methodist Church will be different. No one can tell you the shape of that future. It is currently unimaginable. Knowing this should teach us to be humble and patient.

Right now, I think the United Methodist Church is midway between steps two and three above. We have spent nearly half a century discovering how dysfunctional it is to have disciplinary language prohibiting the ordination of homosexuals, while not having a clear rationale behind that language. Meanwhile, our society has moved to fully accept LGBTQ people in every area of life and every level of leadership. LGBTQ people teach our kids, serve in our military, and compete on our athletic fields. They have been elected as mayors of two of the country's largest cities, are now serving openly in Congress, and, as I write this, are running for President. Like the cover of this book, our church is on an ice floe that is becoming further and further away from the average American.

Instead of seeing 2019 in St. Louis as the place where the United Methodist Church made its decision, we should say that we signed a contract. That contract forces us to participate in a *Love It or List It* type of process. The dust is now in the air and the walls are being moved. The realtor is showing some of our people alternative homes. I have a name for this midway point. I call it the state of Maximum Mess. In the end, some people will love the new UMC, but others will decide to leave it. For everyone, however, there will be disruption.[1]

Circles of Leaving

Currently the majority of clergypersons and congregations are planning to remain within the United Methodist Church, but there are varying degrees of compliance with the adopted Traditional Plan. Several Western bishops and conferences have issued statements that they will not enforce the Discipline's language on LGBTQ issues. Many United Methodist seminaries, colleges, and agencies with LGBTQ faculty and staff, are committed to serve all people without discrimination. The inability of the General Church to force compliance is likely to cause some more conservative elements to become impatient and leave the denomination.

There will also be the expected exodus of people who supported the more progressive "One Church" plan. These departures may be delayed as various components of the Traditional Plan are subjected to legal challenges, and each annual conference decides how it will implement the decisions made at the Special General Conference. I predict, though, that even if the Traditional Plan is only partially implemented, there will be a significant number of members, congregations, and church leaders who will feel forced to leave the United Methodist Church.

It is helpful to visualize this exodus as three concentric circles. In the inner circle are LGBTQ laity and clergy who may leave the church entirely because the institution no longer recognizes the loving and covenantal relationships they have entered into, or because they are being asked to accept a gender identity which they feel is false. Surrounding this relatively small circle is a much larger circle of people who may choose to go with them because they have LGBTQ family members, respected coworkers, and friends, whose personal testimony is more persuasive than the church's teachings on this issue. Claiming that something is doctrine doesn't have the same cohesive power it once did. Meanwhile. the motivating force of personal relationships has grown stronger in the postmodern era.

Then surrounding these two circles is a vast throng that may number a third of the United Methodist Church's total membership. These people view LGBTQ rights as a social justice issue, and they are now making difficult decisions about what form their protest should take. Whatever we feel about the issues, or the scriptures, or the decades that our church has spent going around and around about human sexuality, we dare not casually dismiss those who find themselves in this outer circle. Few social issues have gained as much traction in the last fifty years as LGBTQ rights.

What Would Thoreau Do?

In the weeks following the Special General Conference, I found myself rereading two documents that have great significance for American history. The first was Henry David Thoreau's "On Civil Disobedience" (1849). Thoreau writes that any "government in which the majority rule in all cases cannot be based on justice." This may seem an unlikely statement from someone who fully participated in the democratic process. I think what Thoreau means is that the majority tends to decide what is best for itself, even when that action is unjust. LGBTQ people will always be a minority within the United Methodist Church. It will take something more than a vote of the delegation in a General Conference to fully accept them.

Thoreau writes that civil laws can be properly passed by legitimate authorities, but still be morally wrong. When this happens, individuals of conscience are required to disobey those laws. For Thoreau, doing the right thing meant refusing to pay that part of his taxes that supported the Mexican-American War, which he saw as a blatant land-grab by our government. He also engaged in civil disobedience to protest the return of runaway slaves to their masters. When bishops, agencies, and conference boards of ordain ministry, refuse to follow the legitimately voted-upon sections of the Discipline, they act as individuals of conscience following in the footsteps of Thoreau. When a congregation chooses to withhold a portion of its apportionments (mission share) to the General Church to protest its actions, it is acting as Thoreau did, when he went to jail rather than provide tax revenue for what he considered an unjust war.

Someone else who followed in Thoreau's footsteps was Dr. Martin Luther King. His Letter from Birmingham Jail (1963) was written to explain his leadership and participation in acts of civil disobedience. He considered the laws and customs that segregated American society by race to be unjust and immoral. King writes, "Injustice anywhere is a threat to justice everywhere," and quotes Saint Augustine, saying, "an unjust law is no law at all."

Both Thoreau and King found themselves taking actions they knew to be unpopular. People do not wrestle with the complexities of the LGBTQ issue because they hope their involvement will be appreciated. There is always a danger that when you study a relevant issue, you may awaken a portion of your conscience that previously lay dormant. This may lead to an action. This civil or church disobedience is likely to be misunderstood by others.

Dr. Martin Luther King thought long and hard about what it meant for a Christian leader to be involved in acts of civil disobedience. King used his time in the Birmingham jail to succinctly state the steps we must follow whenever we act against what the majority considers to be a legitimate law.

- Step 1) We must collect all the facts and fully understand the justice issues surrounding the situation.

- Step 2) We must negotiate in good faith with those who take the opposite view and have some power of authority in the matter.
- Step 3) We must engage in self-purification — fasting, prayer, confession, and the study of scripture.
- Step 4) We must choose the appropriate targeted action. It must not be done in anger or with the intent to cause indiscriminate harm.

Following King's methodical steps, those who are considering leaving the United Methodist Church today may find it is not the best way to act against the perceived injustice. They may choose to remain within the United Methodist Church but engage in acts of protest. It is important that we each prayerfully discern, not only where we should stand on the LGBTQ issue, but also what action is justified and appropriate to take.

We May Not See the End

This all is a marathon, not a sprint. Not all of us will live to see the resolution of the controversy surrounding LGBTQ people in the United Methodist Church. The story of Moses and the great wilderness transition came to an end on Mount Pisgah (Deuteronomy 34:1-12). Like all great stories, it is bittersweet. The future lay before Moses. He could look into the Promised Land, but not enter. His role was to guide the people out of slavery and through a transitional period. I've always felt that those who look for some sin to be the cause of Moses not crossing the Jordan, miss the point. Most of the world's greatest leaders were given term limits. Winston Churchill led Britain through World War II, and then was promptly voted out of office. Alan Turing conceived the logic behind the modern computer, and then was discredited, ostracized, and driven to suicide. An ungrateful military complex revoked Robert Oppenheimer's security clearance after he had midwifed us into the atomic era. The list goes on.

The most memorable example, however, is Dr. Martin Luther King. For those of us who see parallels between America's racial divide and the Christian church's long running hatred of LGBTQ people, his legacy is significant. King referred to the end of Moses' leadership on Mount Pisgah, when he said:

> [God has] allowed me to go up to the mountain.
> And I've looked over, and I've seen the
> Promised Land. I may not get there with
> you. But I want you to know tonight, that
> we, as a people, will get to the Promised
> Land. And so I'm happy tonight; I'm not
> worried about anything; I'm not fearing any
> man. Mine eyes have seen the glory of the
> coming of the Lord.
>
> — Martin Luther King's last speech at Memphis, Tenn.
> April 3, 1968

Conclusions

This book has advocated that local church leaders become both informed and intentional in their actions relating LBGTQ concerns. Some of the hurt that haunts the United Methodist

Church today stems from our moving too quickly. In life, leaping before you look works. Sometimes. There are times when taking action before you are ready leads to tragedy. It is often said that deciding when to act is as important as deciding how to act. What we have sought to add to that wisdom is the understanding that significant decisions and actions don't create healthy change overnight. For good or evil, how we on the local level respond to the General Conference 2019 will lead our congregation into a period of transition or wilderness.

In transition, the leaders must come to believe that a healthy decision-making process is more important than any one decision. This first involves learning to listen; that is, being willing to hear the issue from both sides. Second, a healthy process involves providing time for serious thought. Group reflection must take place in a safe space where each person's thoughts are valued. Only then can we move onto speaking and acting.

Even after spending a number of weeks studying this issue, you may still feel some personal frustration. You may be a pastor or church leader who wants to move the congregation in a particular direction, but are failing to get the desired support. It is important to realize that each congregation is a family system built upon interlocking relationships. Change is never a matter of simply getting the majority to think a particular way. Instead, you must note how people relate with each other and build alignment with an agreed-upon vision. You must note people's values and show how the appropriate action connects with what their hearts believe to be true.

You may be still grieving what has been lost, or fearing the future. That is not only normal, but scriptural. The Bible tells one story after another about people having to let go of the past before they could transition to the future. Letting go is a grief process, which involves the five stages of grief outlined by Dr. Elisabeth Kübler-Ross: denial, anger, bargaining, depression, and acceptance. These stages may come in any order or may even be experienced multiple times as you cross the wilderness. Two things remain true: you must lose the past in order to gain the future, and there is no quick exit or easy way to speed up your time in the wilderness.

The good news is not simply that God is good, but that God is intentionally bringing about a just and appropriate future for all of humanity. This continues to be seen in four ways:

- God always listens to our prayers.
- God is always ready to guide our thoughts towards wisdom.
- God still speaks through the scriptures and times of spiritual discernment (Holy Conferencing).
- God still acts to make disciples for the transformation of the world.*May this God bring you peace and grace in this time.*

STAY CURRENT WITH *HELP! MY CHURCH IS LEAVING ME*

Updates can be found at: https://notperfectyet.com/resources Not Perfect Yet Publishing's newsletter will also provide links for free eBooks and discounted future editions. Subscribe at www.eepurl.com/dgBDqL You may unsubscribe at any time. Also, you may leave a review at: www.amazon.com/Help-My-Church-Leaving-Me/dp/0999768743/

Resources by Chapter

Introduction

1. Baptismal Covenant III, The United Methodist Hymnal p.45

1. What Just Happened?

1. GC2019 Advance Daily Christian Advocate publication is available at http://www.umc.org/who-we-are/gc2019-advance-edition-daily-christian-advocate
2. 2016 Book of Discipline, Par. 161
3. Preface to the Social Principles p. 105, 2016 Book of Discipline
4. From the United Methodist Book of Worship, Marriage Service
5. 2016 Book of Discipline, Par. 105

2. What Would Jesus Hear?

1. Reality Check 101: New Paths for a Changing Church by Bill Kemp, outlines several processes for bringing lesser heard voices out in small groups.

3. The Art of Listening

1. Dr. Albert Mehrabian, professor emeritus of Psychology at UCLA, wrote several papers advocating the 7%-38%-55% rule. One caveat is that this rule only applies when the message involves emotion.
2. *"Filter bubble"* is a term that was coined by internet activist Eli Pariser. See https://en.wikipedia.org/wiki/Filter_bubble

4. What Would John Wesley Think?

1. Paragraph 104, "The General Rules of the Methodist Church," The 2016 United Methodist Book of Discipline
2. Wesley did have an appreciation for the philosopher John Locke who paved the way for enlightenment understandings of individual freedom.

5. Thoughts on Wilderness

1. Managing Transitions: Making the Most of Change by William Bridges is a helpful book about transition and the wilderness experience.

6. Reality, Loss, and Spirituality

1. The Church Transition Workbook by Bill Kemp is geared towards helping PPRC committees navigate transition.

7. What Would Paul Say?

1. For more on the changing definition of sin see, Speaking of Sin: The Lost Language of Salvation by Barbara Brown Taylor
2. For more about Paul's apocalyptic mindset, see Paul: The Mind of the Apostle by A. N. Wilson.

8. What's Love Got to Do with It?

1. The Righteous Mind: Why Good People Are Divided By Politics and Religion by Jonathan Haidt provides some useful insight into why conservatives and liberals approach social issues differently.

9. What Then Should We Do?

1. Conflict may be another word for disruption. The Arbinger Institute provides two helpful resources for understanding conflict, The Anatomy of Peace: Resolving the Heart of Conflict and Leadership and Self-Deception: Getting Out of the Box.

Fixing Church 7.0: *A Seven Week Study*

Fixing Church's seven short chapters are geared towards getting people talking. The book/group study starts at the beginning -- What did Jesus really say about Church? Why is his first message to a congregation all about *blessing*? How does my church bless me? Do I bless others when I spend my time in church? And most importantly, *How can my congregation become* **Church** *with a capital* **C**?

Reality Check 101: *New Paths for a Changing Church* - This workbook provides a practical, step by step, process for implementing needed change in any congregation.

The Church Transition Workbook: *Getting Your Church in Gear / A guidebook for difficult transitions*

Provides a process for congregational dialogue and implementing change. Designed for use by leadership teams, PPRC, during pastoral change, as well as, on goal setting retreats and for groups meeting to chart a new course for their congregation. (Only available in print from Not Perfect Yet Publishing)

Check out Bill's weekly word blog at www.billkemp.info
His books can also be found at:
www.amazon.com/author/billkemp

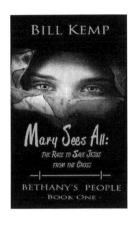

Mary Sees All: *The Race to Save Jesus from the Cross* - is the first in a series of fast paced Christian novels set in the middle east during the first century. The little village of Bethany, near Jerusalem, is home to Martha, the pragmatic clan leader, Mary, the wandering mystic, and Lazarus, who as a zealous teenager had trained to be a terrorist. The books also introduce us to Mark, the African born refugee who witnesses the growth and struggles of the first Christians, and in time writes a best selling account of Jesus's life.

I Believe: *A Full-length Lenten Drama* - Play opens with darkness, a single light, and a weeping woman. This is the small village of Bethany, adjacent to the holy city of Jerusalem. Jesus has just been betrayed and arrested. Two of his disciples now creep towards this house, seeking refuge and bringing the bad news to Lazarus, Martha, and Mary. The next

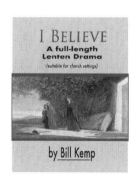

thirteen scenes gradually move the viewer from darkness to light, from fear to inspiration. **For Production Help and Questions email contact@billkemp.info**

About the Authors

Darrell Coats is a native Texan and is presently an extension minister, specializing in working with conflicted congregations and helping local churches navigate difficult transitions. He has had training in Bowen Systems Theory and Mediation. Darrell has been married to Catherine Coats for over 45 years, a partner in a prominent Social Security Disability firm, Coats & Todd. He is the father of two grown sons, Chris and Zachary, and has two grandchildren.

Joe Fort is a fourth-generation United Methodist pastor from the Texas Annual Conference. His years of ministry have encompassed a wide variety of settings: associate pastor in Houston, a startup congregation in a blue-collar bedroom community, East Texas county seat church, 17 years as lead pastor in two

different congregations of roughly 4000 members, and district superintendent. He presently serves as the lead pastor at Lakewood United Methodist Church in northwest Houston. He has been married to his spouse Margaret for 35 years. They delight in their four grown children and (so far) six grandchildren.

 **Roger Grace** is a retired Elder in the West Ohio Conference of the United Methodist Church. He served primarily rural, "Town & Country" churches for 18 years before serving a seven-year term as District Superintendent of Athens District, and Assistant to the District Superintendent for 10 years. He continues to work part-time as a church consultant helping with visioning and conflict resolution. He has been a delegate to Jurisdictional Conference five times, and a delegate to General Conference three times. He is married to Sue and they have three sons and eight grandchildren.

Bill Kemp is an enthusiastic writer, pastor, and teacher. He is the author of a dozen books targeted at bringing about change in the local church. In 2010, he launched Not Perfect Yet Publishing, as a way to better market this material, publish fiction, and promote the use of drama in worship. He has written numerous plays and three full-length  novels. Bill lives near Pittsburgh PA with his wife, Karen. They have been blessed with two children, a dog, and two cats (one of which may be fictional).

Kathy Moore is a United Methodist pastor from the Iowa Conference living in Indianola, Iowa. She served a total of 15 churches in Iowa for 30 years before retiring in 2018. She loves preaching, teaching, and is passionate about missions and social justice. One of those churches was a member of Reconciling Ministries, with about two-thirds of the members part of the LGBTQ community. She was trained as a TIIMS (Transitional/Intentional Interim Ministry Specialist) and served four churches as an intentional interim pastor. With retirement she considers her next career to be a writer, to include various kinds of non-fiction, novels, mysteries and blogging. She loves writing hymns, with two award-winning selections, and she intends to write hymns, hymn books and a devotional book based on her hymns.

Please help our NPY Authors continue to provide useful content by leaving an honest review at: www.amazon.com/Help-My-Church-Leaving-Me/dp/0999768743/

Leaving a review helps get Bill Kemp and other independent authors to be distributed and recognized in today's competitive book marketplace.

Made in the USA
Middletown, DE
07 November 2019